T0137495

I KNOW HIM

—

RISKING IT ALL SO
THAT ALL MAY KNOW

RACHEL SWEATT

WESTBOW
PRESS®
A DIVISION OF THOMAS NELSON
& ZONDERVAN

ESV: Unless otherwise indicated, all scripture quotations are from The Holy Bible, English Standard Version (ESV). Copyright 2001 by Crossway Bibles, a division of Good News Publishers. Used by permission. All rights reserved.

NIV: Scripture quotations marked NIV are taken from the Holy Bible, New International Version. NIV. Copyright 1973, 1978, 1984 by International Bible Society. Used by permission of Zondervan. All rights reserved.

NLT: Scripture quotations marked NLT are taken from the Holy Bible, New Living Translation, copyright 1996, 2004, 2007. Used by permission of Tyndale House Publishers, Inc. Carol Stream, Illinois 60188. All rights reserved.

WestBow Press books may be ordered through booksellers or by contacting:

WestBow Press
A Division of Thomas Nelson & Zondervan
1663 Liberty Drive
Bloomington, IN 47403
www.westbowpress.com
1 (866) 928-1240

Because of the dynamic nature of the Internet, any web addresses or links contained in this book may have changed since publication and may no longer be valid. The views expressed in this work are solely those of the author and do not necessarily reflect the views of the publisher, and the publisher hereby disclaims any responsibility for them.

Any people depicted in stock imagery provided by Thinkstock are models, and such images are being used for illustrative purposes only. Certain stock imagery © Thinkstock.

ISBN: 978-1-9736-0055-8 (sc)
ISBN: 978-1-9736-0057-2 (hc)
ISBN: 978-1-9736-0056-5 (e)

Library of Congress Control Number: 2017912942

Print information available on the last page.

WestBow Press rev. date: 8/29/2017

Dedication

To Emmett and Easton.
May your love for others and your passion for Christ
be the momentum that carries you all of your days.

To the church.
I hope you are encouraged, empowered, and inspired
by what God has done for you.
It is an honor to share the greatest story ever told alongside you.
Take courage. Stand firm in your faith. Love one another.
Share your story.

Contents

Introduction

Hashing out the Hash Tag

In any epic adventure, community is a vital and necessary component. Nothing is as painfully discouraging as feeling alone on a difficult journey. Throughout this book, you will see the hashtag #IKnowHim, referring to the ministry of the I Know Him online blog community. This community consists of believers who have said *yes* to the challenge of sharing their #IKnowHim stories, and those who have committed to encouraging others by spreading the message of the I Know Him movement online. The hashtag makes it easy for people all over the world to find stories about God on the move with one click. #IKnowHim links believers together with one song of hope, one message of restoration, and love for one very alive God. As you read this book, I encourage you to check out the blog and browse through the hashtag on any social media platform.

If you are longing to know without a doubt that God is here, God is real, and He is good, my hope is that you find the answers you seek as you read through these incredible testimonies both online and in this book. These stories are submitted by people like you and me with families, careers, and a deep love for Jesus. If you are a believer and you do know Him, it is my prayer that the reminders and testimonies within this book will fill you with an overwhelming gratitude for God's movement in your life and that you will be inspired to join the fight against darkness with the word of your own testimony. If you are reading this book, please know that you have been fought for in prayer, and your story has the potential to make an eternal difference. The things of this world will soon fade away, but as we offer our lives as beacons of hope for the hurting—sharing what He has done for us—we can be confident that when all is said and done, we will have accomplished the only thing that matters in this life: giving ourselves that all the world may know Him.

Part 1

The Vision

To Know Him

I could write all the words in the world trying to describe what it means to *know* Him, and would not even come close to describing the extravagant, intimate, bewildering experience a relationship with God is. But one seemingly insignificant day, God asked me to try to accomplish just that. Because it's not about getting the words just right but rather inviting people to join in the experience of what it means to *know* Him. It's about the urgency that we—that I—be bold in sharing stories of our experiences with Him. It's about the value of sharing our testimonies regardless of consequence. It's about unashamedly telling the world what God has done for us. It's an overwhelming task, but God is so faithful to patiently walk with us, step by step. Shortly after beginning my journey with #IKnowHim, I came across an excerpt that excellently describes my feelings on the vastness of what it means to know Him. In his book *Confessions,* Saint Augustine writes:

> You, my God, are supreme, utmost in goodness, mightiest and all-powerful, most merciful and most just. You are the most hidden from us yet the most present amongst us, the most beautiful and yet the most strong, ever enduring and yet we cannot comprehend you. You are unchangeable and yet you change all things. You are never new, never old, and yet all things have new life from you. You are the unseen power that brings decline upon the proud. You are ever active, yet always at rest. You gather all things to yourself, though you suffer no need. You support, you fill, and you protect all

things. You create them, nourish them, and bring them back to perfection. You seek to make them your own, though you lack for nothing. You love your creatures, but with a gentle love. You treasure them, but without apprehension. You grieve for wrong, but suffer no pain. You can be angry yet serene. Your works are varied, but your purpose is one in the same. You welcome all who come to you, though you never lost them. (1.4)[1]

Personally, I do know this incredible God. I've experienced the vastness of His wonders and the depths of His love. I have been given His incomprehensible gift of grace. I have witnessed miracles and felt Him near me when I needed Him the most. And I know many people who follow Him and have lived similar experiences. However, it was the people who *didn't* know Him that God used to reveal this message to me—the message of what it really looks like to *know* Christ—to know that God is here, God is real, and He is good. What does a life look like that is being lived in the midst of a holy God? In Zephaniah 3:17 (ESV) we read, "The Lord your God is in your midst," and I am captivated by the idea that the God of the universe fills the atmosphere around me. But what does this look like in the world in which I live? People are always inspired by stories of God in our midst, stories of those long ago in scripture, but also present-day stories of God on the move. We are moved by supernatural experiences of God hearing our cries and stepping in to act on behalf of those who love Him.

When God initially birthed this idea in my heart, I wrestled with the weight of what it meant to truly know Jesus. In a world that is bombarded with darkness, God revealed to me it was time for the *church* to be light and say, "I *know* Him." Charles Spurgeon once said, "Never did the church so much prosper and so truly thrive as when she was baptized in the blood. The ship of the church never sails so gloriously along as when the bloody spray of her martyrs falls on her deck. We must suffer and we must die, if we are ever to conquer this world for

---

[1] Saint Augustine, *Confessions*, (London, England, Penguin Group, 1961), 23

4

Christ." [2]His statement begs the question that if we are not willing to die, then are we willing to go against cultural norms and claim this land as holy? Are we willing to stand up for those who don't yet know Him and tell the enemy that these people have been redeemed through Christ? Are we willing to fight on their behalf, even when we do not agree with them or necessarily even like them? Pressing further, God used a certain group of people in scripture to communicate this strongly to me. They definitely were not willing to fight for others to know God because they were too wrapped up in fighting for their own perceptions of holiness, an issue we as the church today may know all too well.

My husband and I were on the way to Dallas with our four-month-old baby boy. I had just given him a bottle, and he was giggling and smiling as I sat in the backseat beside him. I grabbed my Bible, seeing an opportunity to spend a few minutes in the Word as we traveled while my sweet babe was content, for the moment. I was reading through a passage in John 8 and came to the part of the chapter where Jesus was being confronted by the Pharisees once again. Just like the villain in a movie, the staunch, stale, and hard-hearted Pharisees arrived with the intent of causing destruction. Jesus boldly declared, "Truly, truly, I say to you, if anyone keeps my word, he will never see death" (John 8:51 ESV). The religious crowd, their anger increasing by the second, gave their rebuttal. "The Jews said to him, 'Now we know that you have a demon! Abraham died, as did the prophets, yet you say, "If anyone keeps my word, he will never taste death." Are you greater than our father Abraham, who died? And the prophets died! Who do you make yourself out to be?'" (John 8:52–53 ESV). The Pharisees, the ones who claimed to know the most about God, now found themselves asking the Messiah, the very one they claimed to live for, "Who are You?"

The Messiah, unwavering, began to speak with words that continue to pierce through the ages.

---

[2] Charles Spurgeon, *Spurgeon's Sermons Volume 06: 1860,* (Ontario, Canada, Devoted Publishing, 2017,) *140*

> Jesus answered, "If I glorify myself, my glory is nothing.
> It is my Father who glorifies me, of whom you say, 'He
> is our God.' But you have not known him. *I know him."*
> (John 8:54–55 ESV)

This crowd, full of individuals who thought they had made loyalty to God their lives, had just had their hearts ripped open, and exposed underneath were dark, empty tombs where no relationship with Him could be found. They didn't know Him. They knew of Him. They preached about Him. They even spoke for Him. They made outward expressions about Him, but they had never experienced Him. They didn't *know Him.*

When I read this passage in the car on December 8, 2015, the weight of those three words Jesus spoke hit me like a ton of bricks. *"I know Him."* I immediately felt God asking me to examine my heart. My life. My experiences. Where was the evidence that I knew Him? Were there moments in my life where I knew that the Lord Almighty was in my midst?

He pressed further. God began to speak to my heart in the beautiful, sacred, silent way only He can. It seemed the weight of the world was on my shoulders as I began to think of all the darkness covering the earth. The people, the lives, the souls who are constantly threatened by evil, wicked intentions, and stories of tragedy and despair. I once heard that although we feel as though this may be one of the darkest, most violent times in history, we may just be hearing more of it for the first time due to the rapid expansion of the Internet and social media. The news of the wicked spreads quickly, but how fast does good news travel? How fast does *the good news* travel? How quickly does the gospel spread from one nation to the next, from one people to the next? Across oceans, across mountains, across national borders, and across state lines, neighborhoods, and backyards. The Lord had me wrestle with these questions, and for a while I honestly felt completely overwhelmed. Then, once again, He spoke to my heart. Through the darkness, through the despair, every life behind every tragedy is looking for *light*. They are looking for *hope*. They are looking for *Jesus*.

What I realized immediately following that moment of clarity, however, was another hard truth. Culturally speaking, no one is "supposed" to say that it is Jesus we need, though He is our only hope. Every few months (or weeks it seems) when something terrible happens, the world bands together and collectively commits to loving better. Loving more. Bringing light and hope back to the world through restoration. This all sounds wonderful, and it is inspiring that people are reminded of the need for love and kindness ... even if only for a second. But the problem with these sentiments is that a person cannot have light to offer the world without Jesus. A person cannot have love if he or she does not have God. First John 4:8 (ESV) says, "Anyone who does not love does not know God, because God is love." The restoration people seek after a tragedy is not merely restoration brought about by human hands but is ultimately redemption. In that same passage John writes, "In this the love of God was made manifest among us, that God sent his only Son into the world, so that we might live through him. In this is love, not that we have loved God but that he loved us and sent his Son to be the propitiation for our sins" (1 John 4:9–10 ESV). Our love, our good intentions, and our hopeful speeches promising to make the world a better place mean nothing without Jesus. Without the cross, there is no redemption.

We long for the day when evil ceases and hope remains steadfast. But the truth is, the restoration we long for comes only through the person of Jesus. In John 16:33 (ESV) Jesus Himself assures us of this: "I have said these things to you, that in me you may have peace. In the world you will have tribulation. But take heart; I have overcome the world." However, presently, it is not extremely popular to say the name of Jesus, much less that you know Him and have a relationship with Him. Despite this, people hear a miraculous story, and they flock to discover the details. They want to know where this incredible thing happened, who was there, and if it might be possible for them to experience too. These stories become a shining beacon of hope, emerging from the rubble of disaster. C. S. Lewis once stated, "If you want to get warm you must stand near the fire: if you want to be wet you must get into the water. If you want joy, power, peace, eternal life, you must get close to, or even into, the thing that has them."[3]

We live in a time in which the existence of God is highly debated. A Gallup Poll from 2005 took this question to surveyors: "Seventy-eight percent of Americans say they are 'convinced' that God exists; another 12 percent think God probably exists, but have 'a little doubt'; and 4 percent think God probably exists, but have 'a lot of doubt.' Only 4 percent think God 'does not exist, but are not sure,' and 1 percent are 'convinced' that God does not exist."[4]

In addition to questioning His existence, our current culture often doubts the mere goodness of God—a God who allows sick babies, horrific accidents, and persecution of those who love Him doesn't make sense to most looking for something to believe in. Divorce is more common than ever, and tragedy is rampant. There are people claiming to be sent from God who spend their days shouting from street corners about sinners and the place reserved for them in eternal darkness. These people scream repentance is required to be spared from hell, but nothing about the freedom that comes with repentance in Christ. They speak nothing of the hope and the joy that comes with choosing to turn from sin and toward a life walking in the light. And are we surprised when people doubt the goodness of a god who only condemns and judges? In the living God, the one true God, there is undoubtedly conviction of sin and the call for repentance. But in Him there is also a Savior who waits to pour out His favor upon us while He covers us in an ocean of *grace*. And this God? He *is* undoubtedly *good*.

Throughout our days of ever-present darkness, the very presence of God is often questioned. We can read numerous accounts of people in the Bible debating God's presence. In Psalm 10:1, even the psalmist contemplates, "Why, O Lord, do you stand far away? Why do you hide yourself in times of trouble?" In spite of our questioning and doubt, God continues to dwell among men. He chooses to pursue us, to love

---

[3] C. S. Lewis, *Mere Christianity*, (New York, New York, HarperOne, 1952), 176

[4] "Americans Have Little Doubt God Exists," Gallup, accessed October 21, 2016, http://www.gallup.com/poll/20437/americans-little-doubt-god-exists.aspx

us, and to show up in our lives in incredible ways, beckoning us closer to His heart all the while.

As I was wrestling with all these issues in my mind, I began to ask God what He would have me do. He began to speak the message of #IKnowHim piece by piece to my heart over the next several months, but it began with one question. I grabbed my journal and wrote down the first words that came into my mind as I began to process what the Lord was doing.

What does it look like to truly know Him? What does it look like to be in the presence of the Almighty One (Psalm 91:1)? God answered me by giving me the task of finding and sharing stories of people who have experienced Him. Stories of people that you and I know that reflect the eternal truth that God is real, God is here, and He is good. The incredible story of the neighborhood grocer's wife being miraculously healed. The moment someone's spouse gets a random check in the mail the day the money they don't have is due. The healing, the provision, the speaking, and the moving of the Living God, never ceasing to show up on our behalf. Romans 8:28 (NIV) says, "And we know that in all things God works for the good of those who love him, who have been called according to his purpose." Every follower of Jesus has a story of God stepping in and rescuing him or her. The body of Christ should be bursting at the seams with stories of people who have seen God work out *all* things for their good. This includes the hard things, the painful things, the joyful things, and the exhausting things. Paul's words in Romans tell us the God of the universe acts on our behalf to make *all* things work together for the good of those who love God.

These are the stories that inspire, that point eyes, ears, and hearts to the God who longs to intervene. The purpose of sharing these stories is to spread the name of Jesus far and wide, faster than a raging wildfire. How incredible would it be to see testimonies of God moving in people's lives being shared over and over, overtaking the spread of darkness that seems to ravage the world! It seems all we hear and see online is war, poverty, brokenness, and despair. What if all of a sudden, stories of people experiencing God began to take over the Internet, conversations at coffee shops, classrooms, and kitchen tables? What if all members of the church began to boldly share the moment that God met them in their greatest need? What if the spotlight began to shift to the evidence that *God is real, God is here, and He is good*?

The Fire

As God began to reveal to me more of this message, He had every intention of simultaneously revealing more of Himself. In his book, *My Utmost for His Highest*, Oswald Chambers says, "God gives us the vision, then he takes us down to the valley to batter us into the shape of the vision, and it is in the valley that so many of us faint and give way. Every vision will be made real if we will have patience."[5] I was desperately trying to steward the vision well, but I was ill-prepared for the many ways God would see fit to shape my own heart. I began a long season of receiving God's rebuke and correction, followed by my repentance as I worked out what it would mean to faithfully carry this vision. I found myself leaning deeper into His Spirit, becoming so keenly aware of the sin hidden away in my heart that I knew God was refining me. He was cutting away everything that could be a hindrance to the work He had for me. After months and months of this cloud of spiritual evaluation, this exhausting season of repentance and refining work, I began to pray for restoration so I could begin to walk step by step in obedience, having cleared away any distraction that might keep me from hearing what He would say.

In the months following, God graciously reminded me who I am to Him. He reminded me that He created me with a purpose, and I was set apart from the very beginning. Jeremiah 1:5 (NIV) says, "Before I formed you in the womb I knew you, before you were born I set you apart; I appointed you as a prophet to the nations." Likewise, Psalm

---

[5] Oswald Chambers, *My Utmost For His Highest: Updated Edition*, (Grand Rapids, Michigan, Discovery House, 1992) 7/6

139:13 (NIV) tells us, "For you created my inmost being; you knit me together in my mother's womb." You see, when God knitted me together, He threw in lots of passion, bold opinions, and big dreams. He seems to have used all the brightest colors of yarn He could find, and in the way only He can, weaved them in a divine order to make the loud, emotionally driven person writing these words. At the center of this woven heart, He also constructed an intense love for people, and more specifically, an unquenchable desire for those people to know God. At the very core of my being is an evangelist.

My three-year-old son was painting just the other day, and I was overcome with joy watching him experience creating something all his own. He was so intentional with every stroke of paint, mixing colors and so carefully moving the paintbrush back and forth. He looked up every fifteen seconds to be sure I was watching so I didn't miss anything he was making. He was so incredibly proud of the work he was doing, and I couldn't have been more proud of him myself. I began to realize that the joy we get from watching our children create is but a speck of dust compared to the joy the Lord experienced when He created those very children—every part of them. Their diverse personalities, quirks, hair color, fingernails, talents, spiritual gifts, and even futures, He created with magnificent elation. And the truth is, He felt the same way about us too—the grown ones, the adults, the ones who have been around the block a time or two. It is so imperative that just as we strive for our kids to know they are unique, chosen, loved, and set apart for abundant life, we remember God wants us to know those truths about ourselves as well. Psalm 147:11 (NIV) tells us, "The Lord delights in those who fear Him, who put their hope in His unfailing love." The Creator takes so much delight in every part of us, and He deemed us worthy of the cross of Christ.

Despite having written the truth of His love on my heart, in my season of rebuke and repentance, I had buried my fire for fear of messing up or missing something or misrepresenting Him. I became so paranoid about becoming too impulsive that I overanalyzed everything, and for a season, this was just what I needed. It felt as if I was walking on eggshells, because I didn't want to appear so outspoken as to be mistaken as unwise. I didn't want to be too bold as to appear overly confident in my own ability. I was gun shy to share what the Lord was telling me to say, even to write, because I didn't want to be embarrassed by my naivety.

Admittedly, these feelings and insecurities stemmed from instances in my past in which the scenario described was reality, and I am confident that God used every single instance to draw me closer, make me more aware, and leading me into deeper relationship with Him. And hear me when I say that I am so sincerely *thankful*. I am so thankful God brought all these things into the presence of His light, where I became painfully aware of my futile thinking and foolish ways. Though I am also confident I will continue to wrestle with each area he brought to light, I am even more confident that God will remain steadfast in His love for me.

In the midst of that heavy and difficult season, I am also overwhelmingly thankful to say that I was not alone for one moment. Throughout this season, God brought several people to speak over me throughout that period of time. A few months into struggling with what God's purpose was in what He'd revealed to me, author and preacher Christine Cain spoke directly to me in a fascinating Q&A during one of her tours by what seemed to be absolute random circumstance. She spoke in response to my question as a messenger and a mentor, sharing things with me only God could know I was wrestling with. One of the many powerful thoughts she shared with me was to be weary of allowing my gifts and talents to carry any ministry I might be a part of. She spoke of the current desire for young people to want the anointing of the Lord, but without any of the suffering. Oil is often made from the crushing of something else. Most people today want the anointing of the Lord, but they are not willing to endure a season of crushing to receive it. The lesson was to be willing to be crushed for the sake of the favor of God. I knew that God was asking me to fight for His anointing. Sure, things were going well and everyone was excited about #IKnowHim, but more than anything, I wanted Him to be pleased. I wanted so badly for God to breathe life into this thing He had handed me, this message He had so clearly given me to share. So, I continued to fight for the anointing. And I sincerely hope with all that I am that I never cease to fight for the anointing of the Lord.

There is nothing more incredible, more exhilarating to me than a life lived with the covering of the Lord. Paul writes in 2 Corinthians 4:17 (NIV), "For our light and momentary troubles are achieving for us an eternal glory that far outweighs them all." Likewise the same author writes in Romans 8:18 (NIV), "I consider that our present sufferings are not worth comparing with the glory that will be revealed in us." Every long season of trial and suffering is worth even one brief second of the Lord's anointing. The glory that Paul taught would be revealed in us is nothing short of the character of Christ Himself. When in our sufferings we draw nearer to God, we cannot help but be transformed by His presence, thus shifting our perspectives. I don't know about you, but if it takes enduring a little (or a *lot*) of grief to experience nearness of God a little more, I am all in. I am all in for a season of temporary suffering in exchange for eternal perspective.

True to His Word, these trials and sufferings I faced brought renewed perspective. As I leaned in closer to Him, I also pressed into the person He had created me to be. Coming from fresh crushing and having any pride I might have cherished kicked to the curb, it was His perfect timing to remind me of those delicate pieces of my heart that made me feel alive, such as my genuine love for people and the way my adrenaline and joy skyrockets when I get to share a revelation from scripture I received during a time of prayer. As I prayed for restoration after the season of crushing, I was reminded of a scripture I read in high school. The moment I first read it, my heart instantly jumped up, and I thought, *That's me! This is exactly how I feel when I get to talk about Jesus!* For about a year before finding this verse, I had struggled with identifying what on earth had gotten into me. Seriously. It seemed all I could think about was sharing what God had done in my life and what He was teaching me. I had a purple flower journal that had little sentences reflecting what God was speaking to my heart covering its pages. And a *lot* of exclamation points! To this day, I feel I still speak in exclamation points, so that hasn't changed! And neither has my excitement for what God is doing in my life and around the world. It has only grown. The verse comes from the prophet Jeremiah, who was chosen to be a messenger of the Lord to the people of Israel. Jeremiah was known as the "weeping" prophet because the Israelites never seemed to heed his warning, and he was almost always begging them to repent for the sake of avoiding the wrath of God, but to no avail. Time after time, God would give Jeremiah a hard word to deliver to His people. And time after time, even though it tore him apart, Jeremiah would faithfully deliver it. In Jeremiah 20:9 (NIV), he writes, "But if I say, 'I will not mention his word or speak anymore in his name,' his word is in my heart like a fire, a fire shut up in my bones. I am weary of holding it in; indeed, I cannot."

This verse affirmed exactly who God was crafting me to be that year in high school, and after a period of evaluation, criticism, confession, and repentance, He let me know that the part of me He had crafted early on was still very much alive. When God reveals something new from scripture or a vision, I get this rush of adrenaline and cannot think of anything else until I have shared it. This fire in my bones at the most basic level always comes down to one thing: the name of Jesus. Nothing gets me more fired up than sharing the incredible things God has done and has yet to do. I am continuously overwhelmed when I get to witness someone taking his or her first step into freedom beginning a new relationship with Jesus. This part of me, this "I have to tell *everyone all the things*" part of me, is something God actually did *on* purpose. And it is for *His* glory, as we are told in Philippians 2:13 (NIV). Of this Paul writes, "For it is God who works in you to will and to act in order to fulfill his good purpose."

Thankfully, through wise counsel and after many, many mistakes, I am learning to walk with a holy confidence that God will show up in strength when I surrender these aspects of my life over to be used *by* Him and *for* Him. Second Corinthians 12:9 (NIV) reminds us of this: "But he said to me, 'My grace is sufficient for you, for my power is made perfect in weakness.' Therefore I will boast all the more gladly about my weaknesses, so that Christ's power may rest on me." When we feel overcome by our weaknesses, one of the most necessary things to do as Jesus followers is to run to our tribe. Our tribe is made up of the people who will love and correct us—those people who have our best interests at heart and a fire for God's truth in their bones. These people will come alongside us in our weakness and lift our heads to steady our gazes on His strength. I had never experienced the weight of this truth before my journey with #IKnowHim.

In my wrestling, I asked God to show me how to surround myself with wise counsel, and He met my need, abundantly answering that prayer. I have an incredible sister and friend in the faith who has been instrumental in the working out of this whole thing God has asked me to be a part of. Time after time, she encourages me and reminds me that I should never keep who God has made me to be out of what He has called me to do. Another member of my tribe is one of the wisest women I know. She is one of those people that when she speaks everyone listens, even though she has never once asked anyone to. I may or may not write down almost everything she says to me (read: I absolutely write everything down), because it is as if the Lord speaks straight through her every time she opens her mouth. This friend never ceases to build me up in the Lord, encouraging me to stand firm and to be obedient to the tasks God has given me, walking confidently in His power despite my youth. My husband, although he usually doesn't share my off-the-charts enthusiasm, always encourages me to keep sharing what God is telling me, even when I am concerned about how the message might be perceived or whom it might offend. Through his encouragement I am often reminded of Galatians 1:10 (ESV), which says, "For am I now seeking the approval of man, or of God? Or am I trying to please man? If I were still trying to please man, I would not be a servant of Christ."

I believe God creates each of us with a unique fire in our bones regarding the ways we engage the world with the Word, and with that, unique people to kindle the fire regardless of our gifting, stages of life, or circumstances. I also am confident that the fire is lit by the breath of God, sending us onward and outward into the world to speak the name of Jesus, declaring what He has done. Fire is mentioned frequently throughout scripture, and I'm convinced that is no coincidence. In every situation, fire is what gets stuff done. Fire was the means by which God chose to signify the dispersal of the Holy Spirit in Acts 2. Fire is what

God used to show the strength of His power when it came to displaying His love for those who were loyal to Him in Daniel 3. Fire is what led the Israelites around the desert as they wandered and also shielded them from their enemies in Exodus 13. Fire changes the atmosphere, warming those around it, and spreads rapidly, all the while overcoming darkness with the light of its flames. This fire in Jeremiah's bones, and mine, is distinctly from God, and with that comes great responsibility. With the message of #IKnowHim, as He refined me and revealed more of this message, it became increasingly apparent that all the stories collected and shared must, without exception, point back to *the* story. Because without *His* story, we wouldn't have stories of our own to tell.

The Story

The story that is a part of every individual's story begins before the world was created. It begins with an eternal God, who always was and always will be (Revelation 1:8). It begins with a breath, as God simply breathed time and space into existence. The story continues as the world and all who inhabit it were created for the sake of worshiping the Creator. We find ourselves in this story the moment that the first two image bearers of God find themselves given the choice to love Him back. They are given the best of the best in the garden of Eden, a heavenly paradise where there is no pain and no shame, and they bask in the physical presence of God. However, as the story goes, there is one stipulation. And Adam and Eve, the first people into whom God breathed life, are given the choice to abide by the boundary set by God or to reject it. Eve falls to temptation, bringing sin into the world from that moment forward. She then shares the moment with Adam, who partakes in rebellion as well.

From that moment on, Adam and Eve are forbidden to dwell in the presence of the perfect and holy God. Their life now includes shame, guilt, evil, and even murder. Their sin trickles down throughout the human race as time moves forward, and temptation is free to roam the earth. The people of God, still chosen to be loved by God, must now face a life of separation from their Creator. The only way to be in communion with a Holy God is to offer a sacrifice, an offering to atone for the sins from which they cannot escape—hatred, jealousy, lust, self-righteousness, pride. Sacrifice after sacrifice after sacrifice. But God had a plan.

There are over three hundred prophecies about the ultimate sacrifice that would cover the sins of man forever, allowing them to dwell in the midst of the Lord once again. The Messiah would be born in Bethlehem (Micah 5:2), of a virgin (Isaiah 7:14), of the line of David (2 Samuel 7:12–13, Isaiah 9:7). His name would be Immanuel (Isaiah 7:14), and He would be rejected by His own people (Psalm 69:8; Isaiah 53:3). The Savior would be betrayed (Psalm 41:9; Zechariah 11:12–13), falsely accused (Psalm 35:11), and led like a lamb to the slaughter, silent as He went to die for the sins of man (Isaiah 53:7). He would be crucified alongside the lowest of the low (Isaiah 53:12), with His hands and feet pierced (Psalm 22:16; Zechariah 12:10), but not one bone was to be broken (Exodus 12:46; Psalm 34:20). But then the Christ, in His power and authority given Him through the Father, would be resurrected from the grave (Psalms 16:10, 49:15), defeating death itself, pouring out atonement for the sins of the world (Isaiah 53:5–12) as He would take His seat at the right hand of God (Psalms 68:18, 110:1).

Just over two thousand years ago, God accomplished that very thing. It began when an angel of the Lord visited a young girl, a virgin named Mary. Mary was informed that she had found favor with God and would deliver the Son of God; she was to give him the name Jesus. Her fiancé, Joseph, was also visited by an angel who confirmed this was indeed the Word of God. When the time came for the baby to be born, the couple happened to be—you guessed it—in Bethlehem, for the census ordered by Caesar Augustus. "She gave birth to her firstborn son and wrapped him in swaddling cloths and laid him in a manger, because there was no place for them in the inn" (Luke 2:7 ESV).

At this point in the story, the gospel of Luke introduces a group of people who were some of the first to tell their story about what God had done since the birth of Christ. They were among the first individuals to spread the name of Jesus far and wide, by means of sharing a personal testimony, a story that told of how the Lord Almighty was in their midst:

> And in the same region there were shepherds out in the
> field, keeping watch over their flock by night. And an

angel of the Lord appeared to them, and the glory of the Lord shone around them, and they were filled with great fear. And the angel said to them, "Fear not, for behold, I bring you good news of great joy that will be for all the people. For unto you is born this day in the city of David a Savior, who is Christ the Lord. And this will be a sign for you: you will find a baby wrapped in swaddling cloths and lying in a manger." And suddenly there was with the angel a multitude of the heavenly host praising God and saying, "Glory to God in the highest, and on earth peace among those with whom he is pleased!" When the angels went away from them into heaven, the shepherds said to one another, "Let us go over to Bethlehem and see this thing that has happened, which the Lord has made known to us." And they went with haste and found Mary and Joseph, and the baby lying in a manger. And when they saw it, they made known the saying that had been told them concerning this child. And all who heard it wondered at what the shepherds told them. But Mary treasured up all these things, pondering them in her heart. And the shepherds returned, glorifying and praising God for all they had heard and seen, as it had been told them. (Luke 2:8–20 ESV)

These shepherds were among the first to see the Christ child and the first to spread the news that He was here. They told how the glory of the Lord had shone among them as the angel of the Lord delivered the incredible message, and all who heard were instantly thinking of one name: *Jesus*. One of the things I love most about this passage is not just that it was the first recorded time someone shared a story about their experience with Christ, but the God who deemed these people worthy for such a monumental moment in history were people others would have considered exceedingly unworthy. In that culture, shepherds were seen as the lowest of the low. Because their profession involved unclean animals, they were also considered unclean. And because they were considered "unclean," they were not allowed to go to the temple to worship or even partake in any ceremonial cleansing. They were isolated by the nature of their career, their presence generally overlooked by society, and spent most of their time in fields left to the outdoor elements and their livestock. But to God they were a crucial part of His plan. They were seen. And they were elected to become the first heralds of the Savior's birth. In the dark of the night, the glory of God met them face-to-face with the best news ever spoken from the lips of heaven.

This tiny babe, who was the Savior of the world, began to grow, and after thirty years of life, Jesus was baptized by John the Baptizer. At Jesus's baptism, the gospel of Luke records another incredible moment.

> Now when all the people were baptized, and when Jesus also had been baptized and was praying, the heavens were opened, and the Holy Spirit descended on him in bodily form, like a dove; and a voice came from heaven, "You are my beloved Son; with you I am well pleased. (Luke 3:21–22 ESV)

From this moment on, Jesus begins preparing for His overwhelming finale, the pinnacle moment of His story on earth. He spends time in the desert preparing for His ministry and is tested by the enemy, experiencing for Himself the warring of flesh and spirit. After leaving the desert, He "returned in the power of the Spirit to Galilee, and a report about him went through all the surrounding country" (Luke 4:14 ESV). Jesus began teaching, calling disciples, and performing miracles and wonders. News about Him spread far and wide. He taught of the love God had for His people and the way those who love Him back should live. Jesus soon had a large following, and soon after came countless enemies. This talk about eternal life through a Messiah was not well received by all, and those in authority worked against Him until one day, Christ was brutally beaten and nailed to a cross to die. What His accusers didn't know, though, was that this was not the end of His story, no. The Savior of the world had come to die not by their hands but in His own willingness to lay down his life for the sins of the world. The darkest day in history had dawned, and the sun had set on the Messiah, bloody and accused. His body was placed in a tomb, with a large stone in front of it, guarded by Roman soldiers. It looked like the end of a story, the end of His story. But in the way only God can, He spoke life into a story that completely reeked of death. He spoke brilliant light into a darkness more dense than in the ocean depths. The next morning, when friends of Jesus came to mourn, they were instead astonished to find the stone had been moved and the tomb was empty! An angel of the Lord was again on the scene, proclaiming yet even more incredible news:

> But the angel said to the women, "Do not be afraid, for I know that you seek Jesus who was crucified. He is not here, for he has risen, as he said. Come, see the place where he lay. Then go quickly and tell his disciples that he has risen from the dead, and behold, he is going before you to Galilee; there you will see him. See, I have told you." So they departed quickly from the tomb with fear and great joy, and ran to tell his disciples. And behold, Jesus met them and said, "Greetings!" And they came up and took hold of his feet and worshiped him. Then Jesus said to them, "Do not be afraid; go and tell my brothers to go to Galilee, and there they will see me." (Matthew 28:5–10 ESV)

These women, these friends of Jesus, immediately ran to tell the others. You see, when God does something miraculous, it should make us want to immediately *go tell somebody—anybody!* If you have had a moment in your life, an experience with the Lord Almighty being in your midst—you might have felt a little bit like they did. These women were filled with *fear* and *great joy*. Something I have learned is that when I can feel God on the move, I am filled to the brim with fear and overflowing with great joy.

One dark night after leaving the gym, I decided to put on some worship music and go on a drive before returning home. The sun was just beginning to set, and if you know me, you know watching a sunset is one of my love languages. Every time I get the privilege of gazing upon one, my breath is taken away, my heart is steadied, and my soul silently sings. Those few short minutes were like a breath of fresh air. The promises of God being sung over me through the speakers ushered in a new atmosphere in my car and in my life. I felt God begin to speak to my heart—not audibly, but I knew without a doubt what He was saying. I prayed to Him, speaking the concerns of my heart, my anxieties, and my desperate plea for Him to show up. My heart was heavy, my flesh was tired … and I knew the enemy was camping out on me. In an instant my attention shifted to the work of the enemy in my life, and I felt God prompting me to vocally acknowledge Jesus's victory over Satan, claiming His promises, His victory, and His power. I began to feel my face flush, my body heated by the fierce tone in my voice as I exclaimed promises and verses from scripture that I had no idea were written on my heart, but were in fact hidden there for just this moment. As I was yelling into the air, telling the enemy he had no place in my life, I felt the Holy Spirit empower me to vocally reclaim my territory from Satan—to tell him specifically that he could not have my family, my church, my ministry. He was not going to come at my people, the ones I love most. I was fighting a supernatural battle, and by the grace of God and the power of the Holy Spirit, I was winning. I was throwing up my shield of faith to extinguish his flaming arrows and assailing Satan with the sword of truth (Ephesians 6:10–17), and friends—it felt *good*. Though my body was warm, a great chill came over me, and I knew the very presence of God was with me.

He met me in the most seemingly random place, spoke straight to my heart, and empowered me to keep going in obedience and strength. And not just to keep going, but to fight the good fight with the adrenaline of the Holy One pulsing through my veins. That night I felt as if He was in the passenger seat, cheering me on in supernatural power, reminding me of the victory that lies ahead, the victory that began on that dark day of crucifixion when it seemed His story was over.

All those prophecies, the shepherds, the infant babe, the cross, and the empty grave are all part of God's great story—the story of redemption. Because of the sin of man, the ultimate sacrifice had to be made. A spotless lamb slain must be slain so that the price of sin could be paid forever. This Jesus, God's only Son, was that Lamb. The spotless Lamb who stepped down from heaven became a servant and died a sacrificial death on the cross so we could be with Him forever. Jesus's death on the cross bridged the gap from sin and death to a life abundant.

Each one of us is offered the choice to partake in His story when we encounter Jesus. The name of Jesus alone holds the power to set us free, and it is by His name that we are saved. God gave the initial instructions to spread the name of Jesus to a group of people who were outcasts of society and had no roof over their heads at night. God had come to meet with the very individuals who society declared were not allowed to meet with God in the temple. This is why it is our job, our privilege, to tell the world that we know Him. Imagine everyday people, with families and careers, broken hearts, and heavy burdens, experiencing for the first time a God who is willing to bend down from heaven and *meet us here*. Just as the shepherds shared of their encounter with Him, it is our responsibility to herald the good news as well—the news that God sees us as worthy, redeemed, and beloved! When people far and wide begin to hear stories of God intervening in people's lives, the atmosphere will change as onlookers stop in wonder, their minds suddenly shifted to the One who longs to meet with them as well.

July 21, 2009, is the day that my world got turned upside down and shattered into a million pieces. It was the last day I'd ever hear my son's voice and feel the weight of his body in my arms. No more "I love you mosts," hearing him call me mama, or listening to him tell me all about how he wanted to be a pilot one day.

The reality of him no longer being here really didn't begin to sink in until a couple of months after his accident. I was tucked away in a closet, sobbing at the fading memory of my sweet boy's precious voice. It had been two months since I had last heard him, and I was trying desperately to recall any detail of how I remembered him sounding. Unfortunately, I had no video of him. Life had been busy with having babies only eighteen months apart, and iPhones weren't quite around yet.

My mom eventually found me in that dark closet and convinced me to go for ice cream with my two-year-old daughter. On the ride to the ice cream shop, my sweet girl began singing her big brother's favorite song, "I'm in the Lord's army," word for word! She had never sung it before and hadn't heard it since her brother had gone to heaven. Stunned, I frantically grabbed my phone and began trying to find the record button to capture the moment on video. I had never taken a video on my blackberry before, just thousands of pictures. I couldn't wait to show my husband that our daughter was singing Will's favorite song, the song he would march tirelessly around the house singing. I knew that if I didn't record it, he may not believe me, and kids never seem to perform on command.

While my mom took Maria in for a scoop of ice cream, I decided to wait in the car, seeing that I was a mess and wanted to try and find the video I had just taken of her. What I discovered on my phone that night still leaves me covered in chills to think about. Much to my surprise, there were over thirty videos recorded on my phone. I had only taken one.

Not knowing which one was of my daughter singing the song, I clicked on a file and heard the sweetest, most incredible sound saying, "*Mom*! Look, Mom, I-I-I *see* you, Mom, loooook, I *see* you!' Completely stunned, totally overwhelmed, and overjoyed, I continue clicking on video after video of my sweet boy recording himself, and his dad and me, asking us to "say cheeeese."

All of those times that he had my blackberry, and I thought he was just pretending to take photos on my phone, he had actually been documenting videos—lots and lots of videos radiating the sweet sound of his precious voice, complete with his stutter he had when he was excited. I never had any new photos when he was done playing with my phone, so I figured he was just pretending to take pictures because he saw me taking them so often.

There is no denying that discovering those videos that very night was no coincidence. I could have found them any other time, but I didn't. I could have clicked first on any of the thirty videos, but the very first file I randomly chose was of my boy saying, "Mom, look, I see you."

There is no doubt that God orchestrated every last detail for me that night. From my mom convincing me to go for ice cream; to my daughter singing Will's favorite song out of the blue; to me hearing his voice just moments after grieving the grim reality that it was becoming a fading memory.

God's presence was palpable as I clicked on each video, growing more overwhelmed with each one. He cares. He longs for us to cry out to Him so that He can show up in the most intimate way. Reminding us that He loves us, He is with us always, even in those dark closets we tuck away in. He *sees* us even there.

#IKnowHim story submitted by Patcine McAnual
The Will to Choose
www.thewilltochoose.com

Part 2

The Battle

The Struggle is Real

The story of redemption, the story of Christ, has been the underlying target of an unseen battle that actually began in the garden of Eden. The villain of the story, Satan, knew God created man with the ability to choose to love God or to deny Him. Satan knew he could never defeat God. The power of his darkness was absolutely nothing compared to the power of the glory of the Lord. The enemy decided that if he could not have the Creator, he would go after His creation. If Satan couldn't touch the Father, He would go after His children. He determined to do everything in his power to prevent the children of God from hearing, believing, and especially living in the power of the cross. The power of the cross brought freedom from sin, freedom from death, and life eternal with God. Since man was created, Satan has made it his mission to destroy the church, to hinder the spread of the gospel, and to stifle the flames of those living passionately in the name of Jesus. But the cross of Christ is the one thing in the history of the world that changed everything for the past, the present, and the future.

I recently heard a story told by author and teacher Ravi Zacharias about Napoleon Bonaparte, regarding a discussion with his generals about his plans to conquer every known nation. With his maps spread out on the table, he pointed to a red dot on a map and told his comrades, "If it were not for this red dot, I could conquer the world!" That little red dot was the British Isles, and the British were key in the turning point battle of Waterloo, which ended his tyranny. Ravi then explained that this is exactly what Satan says about the cross of Christ. "If it were not for that one red dot in time, I could have the world!" But thanks be to God for that red dot in time because it has paid the price for our darkest of sins, leaving Satan with absolutely nothing to condemn for those that believe in Him.

Since Satan cannot change the story of the cross, He attempts to change *our* stories. He masterfully crafts temptations and waits in the shadows to attack those on the fence of really believing Jesus, those who are lingering to know Him. For those who already know Christ, Satan is constantly warring against our spirits, using what is appealing to our flesh to lure us away from our love for God. Jesus Himself describes this vividly in John 10:10 (ESV), "The thief comes only to steal and kill and destroy. I came that they may have life and have it abundantly." Likewise, Jesus exposes Satan's intentions in 1 Peter 5:8 (NIV) when He says, "Your enemy the devil prowls around like a roaring lion looking for someone to devour." It is no coincidence that those running hard after Christ seem to be constantly fighting invisible opposition. The reality is that they are doing incredible kingdom work, serving and effectively sharing in the ministry of the gospel. This makes them one of them most targeted opponents of the enemy. This opposition comes in many forms. Sometimes Satan uses illness to persuade believers to doubt their faith. He also cloaks himself in the temptation to despair, perhaps after tragedy or trial. His attacks can be subtle, as we slowly lose our focus or momentum with an idea or task God has assigned to us. These attacks can also come swiftly, seemingly out of nowhere, when we may be more vulnerable. Either way, we can be assured that he is very real, and so is his longing for us to be thwarted from living a life pleasing to God.

There are several instances in scripture in which we get a glimpse of this spiritual warfare. The most prominent example that comes to mind is the story of Job, a man whose loyalty to God made him the perfect target. "In the land of Uz there lived a man whose name was Job. This man was blameless and upright; he feared God and shunned evil" (Job 1:1 NIV). The verses following describe Job's wealth, his numerous blessings and widespread family, along with more evidence of his righteousness and desire to honor God above all else. The story kicks up a notch when Satan himself comes on the scene:

One day the angels came to present themselves before the LORD, and Satan also came with them. The LORD said to Satan, "Where have you come from?" Satan answered the LORD, "From roaming throughout the earth, going back and forth on it." Then the LORD said to Satan, "Have you considered my servant Job? There is no one on earth like him; he is blameless and upright, a man who fears God and shuns evil." "Does Job fear God for nothing?" Satan replied. "Have you not put a hedge around him and his household and everything he has? You have blessed the work of his hands, so that his flocks and herds are spread throughout the land. But now stretch out your hand and strike everything he has, and he will surely curse you to your face." The LORD said to Satan, "Very well, then, everything he has is in your power, but on the man himself do not lay a finger." Then Satan went out from the presence of the LORD. (Job 1:6–12 NIV)

We see several things in this passage. We are reminded that Job lived a God-honoring life, and God blessed his life and the work of his hands. Interestingly, it is because of this that God allowed Satan to target Job, to attempt to thwart him from the holy life he led. God allowed Satan to use his power to assault all that Job had but forbid him from harming Job himself. The story continued on as tragedy after tragedy befell Job:

One day when Job's sons and daughters were feasting and drinking wine at the oldest brother's house, a messenger came to Job and said, "The oxen were plowing and the donkeys were grazing nearby, and the Sabeans attacked and made off with them. They put the servants to the sword, and I am the only one who has escaped to tell you!" While he was still speaking, another messenger came and said, "The fire of God fell from the heavens and burned up the sheep and the servants, and I am the only one who has escaped to tell you!" While he was still speaking, another messenger came and said, "The Chaldeans formed three raiding parties and swept down on your camels and made off with them. They put the servants to the sword, and I am the only one who has escaped to tell you!" While he was still speaking, yet another messenger came and said, "Your sons and daughters were feasting and drinking wine at the oldest brother's house, when suddenly a mighty wind swept in from the desert and struck the four corners of the house. It collapsed on them and they are dead, and I am the only one who has escaped to tell you!" (Job 1:13–19 NIV)

This is the enemy living out his intent—to kill, steal, and destroy. All of this, and Job responds just the way the story indicates he would: he mourns. But he also reacts just as God knew he would, and he laments in a way that reflects his love for God still remains.

At this, Job got up and tore his robe and shaved his head. Then he fell to the ground in worship and said: "Naked I came from my mother's womb, and naked I will depart. The LORD gave and the LORD has taken away; may the name of the LORD be praised." In all this, Job did not sin by charging God with wrongdoing." (Job 1:20–22 NIV)

Unfortunately, Job's suffering continued. In an attempt to stifle Job's love for the Lord, Satan goes even further, and after getting permission from God, he attacks Job's health. Job finds himself covered in painful sores, from his head to the soles of his feet. As he sits scraping his sores off with broken pottery, his wife questions his loyalty to God.

His wife said to him, "Are you still maintaining your integrity? Curse God and die!" He replied, "You are talking like a foolish woman. Shall we accept good from God, and not trouble?" In all this, Job did not sin in what he said. (Job 1:9–10 NIV)

Satan was unsuccessful in his attempt to lead Job astray, amid the most antagonizing circumstances. His aim was to rid the world of one of the most righteous, most effective people for the kingdom. He knew that if he could tempt this very man, known for his extreme devotion to God, to doubt the goodness of God, he could gain incredible territory. This man had influence. Job was a well-known leader, and for him to turn his back on God would have been an invaluable advantage to the enemy's cause.

This is Satan's intention for us too, for those who are in God. If Satan can spread stories of tragedy faster than testimonies of God's faithfulness are told, perhaps he can lead people to doubt the goodness of God. However, our hope lies in the failure of his attempt. Job remained steadfast in his faith, and his story is one spoken throughout the ages. Because of His confidence in the power that we have received through the Holy Spirit to withstand the enemy, Job inspires believers to remain loyal to the one who allows Satan to wage war on us. God is fully aware of the power we possess when we are given the Holy Spirit, after confessing our sin and our need for a Savior. And that power? Satan knows about it too, and he does everything he can to distract us from using it. But Job was faithful, and he remained steadfast in his love for God. And his love for God, despite every attack, was so deeply rooted in his need for God that he was unwilling to succumb.

Another example of the unseen battle raging within our hearts is found in the gospel of Luke. Jesus, in a conversation with one of his beloved disciples, addresses the warfare raging over Peter plainly and without subtlety:

Simon, Simon, behold, Satan has demanded permission to sift you like wheat; but I have prayed for you, that your faith may not fail; and you, when once you have

turned again, strengthen your brothers. (Luke 22:31–32
NASB)

Let's be honest for a second. No one really *wants* to talk about Satan
wanting to sift us like wheat. But the reality is that this is his objective
for us as long as we walk the earth. We are his constant assignment.
He spends his time trying to silence the church so our faith will be
diminished and he can all the more easily keep those not yet saved from
being saved. Satan will do everything in his power to prevent God's
children from accepting the free gift of grace that Jesus offers to us, the
gift He purchased with His own blood.

Satan knows that Christians are supposed to be sharing the gospel,
doing the work of evangelists, and loving their neighbors as themselves.
He knows believers are the ones who are supposed to be known by their
love for others, their ability to forgive, and their passion for what God
has done in them. What if Satan could prevent believers from sharing
the gospel? What if he could distract believers from doing what God
is asking them to do? What if he could tempt followers of Jesus to
compromise by just being complacent, remaining comfortable instead
of making it their own mission to make disciples? What if Satan could
attack our faith, our belief that God is good and He is here? What if he
gently persuaded us to live in the flesh a little more each day, becoming
known for our love less and less?

If he accomplishes any of these objectives, the rest of his work is
all the easier. But thanks be to God that the only reason Satan strives
so intently is because he knows his time is short: "Therefore, rejoice, O
heavens and you who dwell in them! But woe to you, O earth and sea,
for the devil has come down to you in great wrath, because he knows
that his time is short!" (Revelation 12:12 ESV). The enemy already
knows what is so important for us also to remember. The war has
ultimately been won; Christ has defeated death. At the very end, what
is most important when all is said and done, what we must know this:
no one is greater than God. This bears worth repeating: *no one* is greater
than God. He holds the victory, and although we must struggle and
fight, refining our faith while we wait for him to return—this struggle

is not in vain. That same passage says, "And I heard a loud voice in heaven, saying, 'Now the salvation and the power and the kingdom of our God and the authority of his Christ have come, for the accuser of our brothers has been thrown down, who accuses them day and night before our God'" (Revelation 12:10 ESV).

The authority to rule heaven and earth belongs to God and to God *alone*. Satan may be roaming the earth now, but there will come a day on the kingdom calendar when God determines it is time to rid the earth of our enemy, once and for all. And with one simple *breath,* He will end the accuser, the Father of lies, the enemy of the cross. He will end sin, shame, despair, and temptation once and for all. It is so important to remember that as this supernatural war rages, and we fight our own battles against our flesh and against the evil one, that we are on the winning team. The struggle is real and life is so hard, and Satan is out to sift us like wheat … but God! He uses all things for His good, even what our enemies intend to destroy us with. Second Samuel 22:40 (NLT) echoes this powerful truth: "You have armed me with strength for the battle; you have subdued my enemies under my feet."

God is never surprised, and his work never undone. He is never overwhelmed or hopeless. He wins, and while we put one foot in front of the other, boldly taking the gospel further step by step, with each act of service, continually laying down our selfishness and pride, we are winning too. The Champion of the world is on our side. He once warned Peter that the enemy desired to sift Peter like wheat, but Jesus was *praying for him*, for his faith to remain steadfast. I don't know about you, but I get a knot in my throat when I think about the Messiah praying for *me*. When I consider him praying I would not lose sight of the battle, nor of the victory within His sight, I am left completely *undone*. Jesus's prayer for Peter in Luke 22 was also that he would *strengthen* his brothers. That through whatever experience he may have, he would tell of God's faithfulness and encourage the brothers to stand firm under trial as well.

The Soldier

One of my favorite things about following Jesus is that He knows I cannot do this whole "follow Him" thing on my own. Following Jesus is committing to a life constantly under attack by a spiritual opponent, one who does whatever it takes to create a gap between God and man. However, as a follower of Jesus, He does not send us into battle without giving us the advantage. Just as each moment counts in battle, so does each moment we spend preparing ourselves for battle, perhaps even more than the moments in the battle itself. In every war, there are soldiers with boots on the ground on the frontline. The determining factor in their morale during the battle is directly correlated to their preparation for the fight. This fight is not only for our faith but also for the salvation of others as we pray on their behalf. Our strategy makes an eternal difference in the lives of those yet to know Him. If we are to stand firm under fire and let our testimonies never falter from communicating the grace, goodness, and presence of God in our lives, others will undoubtedly want to know Jesus considerably more than if we were to choose to throw in the towel on a life of following Jesus. They will be intrigued at our resolve, our love in the midst of hate, our ability to forgive, and the audacity with which our lives speak of the grace we have been given. They will ask what is different about us, what is the anchor that holds us steady as life brings storm after storm? These are the moments as followers of Jesus—steadfast and sure of His presence, His goodness, His love for us—we can tell the world wholeheartedly that our unwavering resolve persists because *we know Him.*

Though the enemy is no match for God, we are no match for the enemy if we run behind enemy lines without putting on the armor God has provided for us. In Ephesians 6:10–17 (ESV), the apostle Paul writes in detail how we are to prepare for the fight:

> Finally, be strong in the Lord and in the strength of his might. Put on the whole armor of God, that you may be able to stand against the schemes of the devil. For we do not wrestle against flesh and blood, but against the rulers, against the authorities, against the cosmic powers over this present darkness, against the spiritual forces of evil in the heavenly places. Therefore take up the whole armor of God, that you may be able to withstand in the evil day, and having done all, to stand firm. Stand therefore, having fastened on the belt of truth, and having put on the breastplate of righteousness, and, as shoes for your feet, having put on the readiness given by the gospel of peace. In all circumstances take up the shield of faith, with which you can extinguish all the flaming darts of the evil one; and take the helmet of salvation, and the sword of the Spirit, which is the word of God.

Paul is fully aware of the spiritual warfare that is continually raging and identifies the whole armor of God as necessity in order to withstand the schemes of the devil. He goes on to affirm that our fight is not just against flesh and blood but is supernatural. Soldiers of Christ should go into battle having fastened the belt of truth—standing firm in the true character of God. We must know the heart of God, so as to not be swayed from the fundamental truth that He only desires the *absolute* best for us. Have you ever found yourself more distant from God than you used to be? Almost every time I have felt this way, I realize I have begun to trust in a plan that was my own rather than God's. This essentially means that I doubted His ability to provide *or* started to believe what He was going to provide wasn't going to be what I really desired. Neither of these situations are fruitful, so we must plant our feet firmly in the truth of who God is, *and* who He says we are. Oftentimes the enemy may attack us by condemning us, calling us what we are *not*. We are not good enough. We are not smart enough. We have messed up one time too many. We are unlovable, unforgivable, and irredeemable. None of this is true, but an honest assessment would prove that most, if not all, of us have felt the sting of an arrow from the enemy bearing one of these labels. The only way to fight this is to stand firm in what we *know* to be true. The only way to sustain this attack is to hold fast to what God says about who we are in His Word, His unending love for us displayed by the cross, and His sovereignty over all past, present, and future circumstances.

Another critical piece of armor is the breastplate of righteousness, which is strategically placed over the heart. In Proverbs 4:23 (HCSB), the author writes, "Guard your heart above all else, for it is the source of life." The New International Version words it this way, "Above all else, guard your heart, for everything you do flows from it." The heart is clearly a big deal physically, but spiritually it is everything. Everything we do and how we do it is determined by the condition of our hearts. We also see this in Luke 6:45 (NIV), "A good man brings good things out of the good stored up in his heart, and an evil man brings evil things out of the evil stored up in his heart. For the mouth speaks what the heart is full of." This is not an easy pill to swallow. What have you been storing up in your heart lately? What kinds of things have we been storing at the heart of our nation? No matter what our self-evaluation reveals, the truth remains that our hearts are the source of whatever lives we are living. And we must put on the breastplate of righteousness to shield them from the enemy. Putting a shield of righteousness over our hearts to protect them from anything not of God (especially those seemingly tiny compromises that just sneak past any filter we may have) leads to an increased sensitivity to the Spirit's leading. These moments in which He may be prompting us to pray for someone, to share what He is doing in our lives, or to offer encouragement is much more readily discerned when our hearts are not invaded by flaming arrows.

Likewise, Paul writes of walking confidently in the readiness of the gospel of peace. I recently had an incredible conversation with some sweet, God-fearing women in my life. In discussing what this phrase meant, we talked through different scenarios and what each of us felt like it meant to us, regarding our own experiences. The underlying theme in all of our answers was that knowing that Jesus has saved us gives us the ability to stand firm in a supernatural peace, ready for whatever may come. Knowing that at the end of the day, we are held by the Champion of the world brings incredible peace. The Father sees us, He knows us, and He will never leave us—we are worth too much to Him. This revelation can be life changing. Things may be extremely difficult in our lives. We may even be uncertain of our futures, but having not having any doubt that things really will be okay is invaluable. And not just in the "everything will work out" sense, because honestly that is not always the case, at least while we remain this side of heaven. However, we can be confident that when all is said and done, *we will have Jesus*. And Jesus is all we need. He is all we need to keep marching here, one foot in front of the other, through the fire of war until we are delivered from the fire by whatever means necessary to bring Him glory.

While we are marching, one thing we must always take up in battle is the shield of faith. As God was refining me in the months leading up to the writing of this book, I had a firsthand experience with using my shield of faith in my own fight against the enemy. I became increasingly aware of my sin, and all the ugliest parts of my heart were revealed over a period of time, one right after the next. The enemy certainly had a hand in this, but each time I heard him whisper something about my sin, I heard a voice more powerful say, "Nope, that is *mine*. I have *paid* for that." God used a dear friend in my life to paint this incredible picture of using our shields of faith to prohibit the enemy's malicious attempts to discourage us, especially in our callings, from making their way into our hearts. And while we grow our faith as we raise our shields, He reminds us that this is exactly why He sent His Son to die. This means my salvation and the works I would potentially do for Him would never be dependent on myself, but on the work done by Jesus, and all that was accomplished on the cross. Jesus said, "It is *finished*" (John 19:30 ESV), not, "It is finished … until Rachel messes it up or opens her mouth again." (And all the people who know me said *amen*.)

Every time I heard His voice, every time He reminded me He had already paid for my life, every time I claimed the grace that dripped down from the cross as my own … I raised my shield of faith a little higher. This is crucial in going into battle; in doing whatever it is that God is asking you to do; and in being bold in sharing your own personal testimony. Satan will throw *all the things* at you in order to keep you from doing the work to which you have been called. Every time you feel an arrow of condemnation, shame, or judgment fly by your head, raise your shield of faith a little higher, and tell Satan to *back off* because you are *His*, and nothing will ever change that.

In remembering what God has done for us, Paul reminds us also to put on our helmets of salvation. Our helmets protect what we know, and what we know is that *we are saved*. It doesn't matter how we feel, what our circumstances may be, or how badly we have messed up. If we belong in God, there we will stay. We must know beyond a shadow of a doubt that though the enemy may attempt to ensnare us and our sin may entangle us, Satan will *never* snatch us from the hand of God. In John 10:28 (NIV), Jesus reassures us of this: "I give them eternal life, and they shall never perish; no one will snatch them out of my hand." Jesus freely gives us eternal life. We did nothing to earn it, and we can do nothing to lose it. If we stand firm in our salvation, any foothold Satan may have had in our hearts crumbles under his grasp.

Last, Paul describes the only offensive weapon within the whole armor of God, the sword of the Spirit, which is the Word of God. Here Paul is describing that the Bible, God's inherent truth is available for us to seek and abide by. In regard to its ability to assist us in the battle, Hebrews 4:12 (NIV) tells us, "For the word of God is alive and active. Sharper than any double-edged sword, it penetrates even to dividing soul and spirit, joints and marrow; it judges the thoughts and attitudes of the heart." The scriptures are not just words written thousands of years ago, but they are living and active. The words of scripture pierce beyond the flesh, into our very souls. Hebrews 4:13 (MSG) describes it this way: "Nothing and no one is impervious to God's Word. We can't get away from it—no matter what."

We fight the supernatural battle with the Word of God because with it we can discern the motives of the enemy and align what is really true with what God tells us is true. I will be honest in saying I often fall short when it comes to memorizing God's Word. I know quite a few verses that I memorized when I was young, but up until the last two years of my adult life, I had never taken up the discipline of writing it on my heart. Just two years ago, I joined a mentor group, and part of our curriculum was to memorize scripture each month. Every year after, with a different group, I am continuing that challenge, and the experience has been incredible. When we take the time to *do the* work, read what God has to say to us, store it up in our hearts for the future, and are able to spout it out from the depths of our souls with conviction and the authority given us by the Holy Spirit, Satan *trembles*. Why? Because even he knows the power it holds. He knows the reason we are given only one offensive weapon is because that is *all we need*. But if we do not take up the responsibility to study God's Word, how are we supposed to fight the enemy with a weapon we do not know how to use? I encourage you to step out and find a group that studies and memorizes scripture together. If you can't find one in your area, you have an incredible opportunity to start one! Encourage one another, and let there be holy accountability. Learn *how to fight.*

We are not sent into battle without armor, and praise be to God, we are not sent alone either. Just as I mentioned the group with whom I study and memorize scripture, I would encourage you to seek out a group who sharpens your faith, increases your confidence in the Lord, and are constant advocates of what God is doing in your life. These are the people who will ask you what God is teaching you, what you are learning through your prayer life, and with whom have you have been sharing your story. These are the soldiers who march beside us, straight into the flames, and these are the people who will be marching alongside us in victory. Ecclesiastes 4:9–12 (NIV) explains the power in community:

Two are better than one, because they have a good return for their labor: If either of them falls down, one can help the other up. But pity anyone who falls and has no one to help them up. Also, if two lie down together, they will keep warm. But how can one keep warm alone? Though one may be overpowered, two can defend themselves. A cord of three strands is not quickly broken.

Are we getting the picture? We are here to join up with our fellow soldiers and fight the good fight (1 Timothy 6:12). We were never intended to withstand the devil's schemes alone. We have been charged to put on the whole armor of God, stand with our brothers and sisters, and take the enemy *down*. Our strength comes from knowing that God goes before us and His church is with us. We fight against darkness when we love others. We overcome selfish ambition when we serve those God has entrusted to us. We wage war against hopelessness when we share what God has done in our lives. We succeed when we claim the victory He has already won.

Therefore, since we are surrounded by such a great cloud of witnesses, let us throw off everything that hinders and the sin that so easily entangles. And let us run with perseverance the race marked out for us, fixing our eyes on Jesus, the pioneer and perfecter of faith. For the joy set before him he endured the cross, scorning its shame, and sat down at the right hand of the throne of God. Consider him who endured such opposition from sinners, so that you will not grow weary and lose heart. (Hebrews 12:1–3 NIV)

The Art of War

In his book *Letters to Malcolm: Chiefly on Prayer,* C. S. Lewis writes, "Relying on God has to begin all over again every day as if nothing had yet been done."[6] Following Jesus is something that is decided daily, recognizing we are in need of Him more than ever with each sunrise. Likewise, fighting to make His name known is a priority that is made only if it is intentional. We do not put on the armor of God, ready to go into battle in the name of Jesus on accident. We do not prepare extensively for battle without purpose. As sons and daughters of God, we are given the advantage of knowing how we are going to be led to victory through the power of the cross, the prayers of others, and preparing for what is ahead.

When followers of Jesus go out to share what God has done for them, thus entering into the unseen battle, they are confident that the same God goes before them and walks alongside them, and His power and presence reside in them. The spiritual warfare that rages over the cross of Christ and all those believing and unbelieving is not a war won with guns and bombs but with the power that resides in each of us as a result of Jesus indwelling our hearts. Second Corinthians 10:3–4 (NIV) discusses our ability to war against the unseen. "For though we live in the world, we do not wage war as the world does. The weapons we fight with are not the weapons of the world. On the contrary, they have divine power to demolish strongholds." The divine power about which Paul writes is first mentioned in Acts 1:8 (NIV), where the disciples experienced the power of the Holy Spirit for the first time since Jesus's

---

[6] C. S. Lewis, *Letters of C.S. Lewis,* (New York, New York, HarperCollins, 1966) 220

crucifixion. "But you will receive power when the Holy Spirit comes on you; and you will be my witnesses in Jerusalem, and in all Judea and Samaria, and to the ends of the earth." Theyer's Greek Lexicon mentions one definition of the word *witnesses* here as "a witness (one who avers, or can aver, what he himself has seen or heard or knows by any other means)."[7] By the power of the Holy Spirit, we are given the ability to fight the good fight by testifying to what we have *seen* or *heard*.

The same power that enables us to be bold witnesses to what God has done also gives us divine strength to live out our daily lives with intense focus and energy, increasing our effectiveness in bearing witness. First Corinthians 12:4–11 (NIV) describes the gifts that we are each uniquely endowed with, by the power of the Holy Spirit. These gifts take what God has given us a natural ability for and makes them worthy of supernatural natural warfare by means of using them for the common goal of sharing the gospel:

> There are different kinds of gifts, but the same Spirit distributes them. There are different kinds of service, but the same Lord. There are different kinds of working, but in all of them and in everyone it is the same God at work. Now to each one the manifestation of the Spirit is given for the common good. To one there is given through the Spirit a message of wisdom, to another a message of knowledge by means of the same Spirit, to another faith by the same Spirit, to another gifts of healing by that one Spirit, to another miraculous powers, to another prophecy, to another distinguishing between spirits, to another speaking in different kinds of tongues, and to still another the interpretation of tongues. All these are the work of one and the same Spirit, and he distributes them to each one, just as he determines. (1 Corinthians 12:4–11 NIV)

---

[7] Joseph Henry Thayer, D.D., *A Greek-English Lexicon of the New Testament*, (Edinburgh, T. & T. Clark, 1890) 392

We all have talents, dreams, and passions. What makes them eternally effective as spiritual gifts is when they are empowered by the Holy Spirit to work supernaturally toward the common goal of Christ. This comes into play when we use our creativity or our intellect to share the love of God with others. When we use our musical abilities to remind people they are loved, or when we teach our students with the end in mind, that they were made with a purpose and that nothing is left to chance. Imagine a world in which people's eyes were opened to see that there is much more to life than just surviving day to day—a world in which people began to hear stories about teenagers who believe that God is with them as they set out to make the world a better place by serving others, using their spiritual gifts of hospitality and prayer. Imagine the church getting a glimpse of what it looks like for members of the body of Christ to serve with supernatural strength in the areas of their gifting—teaching, leading, praying, and loving with fierce intensity. This is the kind of life we are invited into, and it is also one move the enemy never wants believers to use for advancing God's kingdom.

Another strategy Satan does not want believers to use is to believe with authority that the Lord Almighty walks before us, taking down our enemies and making the way for us. The enemy does not want us to pray by claiming the promises of God, because when we speak God's strength into the moment, the atmosphere changes and Satan's power crumbles. When we remember that His Word assures us He goes before us, each step forward is taken in confidence rather than fear. We are bolstered by verses like Joshua 1:9 (NIV), which encourages us to, "Be strong and courageous. Do not be afraid; do not be discouraged, for the Lord your God will be with you wherever you go." Likewise, Satan fights ferociously to keep us from calling upon the Lord, claiming victory through the presence of God like we read in Psalm 18:32–39 (NIV):

> It is God who arms me with strength and keeps my way secure. He makes my feet like the feet of a deer; he causes me to stand on the heights. He trains my hands

for battle; my arms can bend a bow of bronze. You make your saving help my shield, and your right hand sustains me; your help has made me great. You provide a broad path for my feet, so that my ankles do not give way. I pursued my enemies and overtook them; I did not turn back till they were destroyed. I crushed them so that they could not rise; they fell beneath my feet. You armed me with strength for battle; you humbled my adversaries before me.

In addition to going into battle empowered by the Holy Spirit, we must also be careful never to enter the battlefield without the power and the covering of *prayer*. Prayer is our lifeline to God, the means by which we voice our thoughts and petitions to the One who designed us. He longs to hear from us, and He longs for us to experience the fullness of a life empowered by prayer.

One of the most powerful scenes in the New Testament takes place on the evening of Jesus's arrest. Knowing the final hours of His mission are at hand, every moment is used to its full potential. He has only moments until He is betrayed, beaten, led up a hill, and killed without an ounce of dignity, and what does He do? He prays. He prayed for you. He prayed for me. He prayed that we would fight hard faithfully and be righteous and effective in this world. He prayed not that God would remove us from evil and suffering but *protect* us from it while we walk out onto the field of battle. While we walk amid pain, sin, and depravity, we have the prayer of Christ Himself covering us, lobbying for our victory. We find His words over us in John 17:14–18 (NIV):

I have given them your word and the world has hated them, for they are not of the world any more than I am of the world. My prayer is not that you take them out of the world but that you protect them from the evil one. They are not of the world, even as I am not of it. Sanctify them by the truth; your word is truth. As you sent me into the world, I have sent them into the world.

We cannot expect to make it through this minefield of life while maintaining our integrity, bearing fruit, and making it safely to our homeland without the prayers of others lifting us. Similarly, our brothers and sisters marching alongside us need our prayers to cover them, to intercede on their behalf, praying that God would increase their boldness with each step they take. Acts 12:5 (NIV) gives us a glimpse into the power at bay when the church comes together for one another. "So Peter was kept in prison, but the church was earnestly praying to God for him." We cannot miss this—there is too much at risk. Peter was in prison. James, his fellow disciple, his brother in the faith and comrade in the battle, had just been beheaded by King Herod. The day before Peter was to be brought out before the crowd, the church *prayed*. There was Peter, about to die for his faith just as his friend. And Peter was ready. He was empowered by the presence of God and the Holy Spirit. He knew that whether he was beheaded or made free, God was sovereign, and he knew that there were things in the works that were beyond Herod's understanding or control. Peter knew the church was praying.

That night, as the church interceded for Peter, for his protection and for his freedom, an angel of the Lord met him in his prison cell. He broke Peter's chains and led him out of the prison. "When he realized this, he went to the house of Mary, the mother of John whose other name was Mark, where many were gathered together and were praying" (Acts 12:12 ESV). The church had gathered to pray in unity for Peter. This is the example we are to follow as we fight to spread the name of Jesus. When we pray for our brothers and sisters, God moves in remarkable ways. The interesting thing is, we don't always know when God is on the move. We don't know if He will send an angel, move a mountain, or bring healing, just as Peter's friends had no idea their friend would still have his head the next day. But they knew it was their responsibility to pray for him, and it was not only a responsibility but a privilege. In the book of Ephesians, Paul writes, "And pray in the Spirit on all occasions with all kinds of prayers and requests. With this in mind, be alert and always keep on praying for all the Lord's people"

(Ephesians 6:18 NIV). So they continued to pray and believed that God would hear them.

First John 5:14 (ESV) gives us an insight as to why Peter's friends were so intent on praying for Him, and why prayer is so important for our battle as well. John writes, "And this is the confidence that we have toward him, that if we ask anything according to his will he hears us." *He hears* us. Proverbs 15:29 (ESV) echoes this promise: "The Lord is far from the wicked, but he hears the prayer of the righteous." The church can be confident that as we march deeper into enemy territory, fighting to bring light to the darkest places, God hears each and every petition we raise to Him. He does not send us alone, without a lifeline. Prayer gives us strength in the depths of our souls, because it is through prayer that we can call upon the strength of God Himself. "Seek the Lord and his strength; seek his presence continually!" (First Chronicles 16:11 ESV). With the strength of the Lord and the presence of God powering us through the fight, victory is never out of sight.

While we keep waging war with the power of God behind us and the Holy Spirit in us, as well as a blanket of prayer covering us, we must also keep our eyes on what lies ahead. One of the most strategic moves in battle is knowing what lies ahead. True to His character, God does not neglect us in this aspect of the battle either. There are two main things we can expect at the end of every battle. First, we can be assured that there will be *persecution*. While, yes, we have people who love us praying for us and our protection, we must remember that Jesus did not choose to remove evil from us. The prayers of those praying for us are effective in a variety of ways. Sometimes we are physically protected from harm. Other times, protection from evil means our hearts remain guarded and our knowledge of who God is and His love for us remains steadfast. Second Timothy 3:12 (NIV) guarantees us that if we are living our lives for Jesus, we will experience suffering. In the same book, Timothy writes in 2:3, "Join with me in suffering, like a good soldier of Christ Jesus." Paul was no stranger to suffering. And yet here he is, encouraging us thousands of years later to partake in suffering, for the sake of Christ. For any soldier, physical injury is always a risk, not to mention the mental angst that comes with memories of their experiences during their service. Other risks include the possibility of capture, torment, and even death. What is different about being a soldier of Christ, however, is that we are *guaranteed* some sort of suffering. In Matthew 5:12 (NIV), Jesus reminded His disciples that persecution comes hand in hand with a righteous life. "Rejoice and be glad, because great is your reward in heaven, for in the same way they persecuted the prophets who were before you." When we experience persecution, we are given the opportunity to shout the goodness of God from the mountaintop to the world, thwarting the enemy's attempt to trap us in the valley. The phrase *"God is good"* carries a new weight with it when spoken from the mouth of someone who has lost a child, has buried a parent, or has no place to call home. However, it is in these moments the apostle Peter encourages us to use our circumstances as a platform for raising the name of Jesus higher than ever before, as if it were a banner covering our battle wounds: "Yet if anyone suffers as a Christian, let him not be ashamed, but let him glorify God in that name" (First Peter 4:16 ESV). The trials and persecutions we face only make it easier to share our stories about the victories we have in the cross.

Second, praise be to God that just as we are guaranteed suffering, we are promised a prize at the end of the race. At the end of the suffering, we are promised healing and restoration. Psalm 107:19–21 (NIV) encourages us, "Then they cried to the LORD in their trouble, and he saved them from their distress. He sent out his word and healed them; he rescued them from the grave. Let them give thanks to the LORD for his unfailing love and his wonderful deeds for mankind." Psalm 147:3 (ESV) speaks of the same restoration after a season of trial: "He heals the brokenhearted and binds up their wounds." These words from God are like water to a parched heart, medicine to the soul, and life to dry bones. In Philippians 3:13–14 (ESV), Paul leaves us with a challenge to keep our eyes on the prize ahead: "But one thing I do: forgetting what lies behind and straining forward to what lies ahead, I press on toward the goal for the prize of the upward call of God in Christ Jesus." *We must never neglect* to put on the armor of God, move forward to the prize that lies ahead, and walk confidently in the power of God and the prayer of the saints.

I was a newborn follower of Christ at age twenty-three in the summer of 1985. Brother Mack Walls was my pastor, and he asked the small congregation to come out on Tuesday nights and visit people in our area to pray and tell them about what God was doing in our lives. Jumping in with both feet, I showed up. I didn't know really anything about God or the Bible at that time. I remember reading the Old Testament and thinking, *Who names their kid Job?* Anyway, no one was there except Brother Mack; his wife, Ruby; and another new Christian named Ken Harris. Ken was the experienced believer of the two of us. He had been a Christian for a few months. We became the best of friends over the next few months. We started meeting early on Tuesday nights to pray before we went out. Then we would meet at the truck stop on I-10 and order a super large order of fries and talk about everything God was doing in both our lives.

One night it was pouring rain, and Ken and I went to the truck stop and were waiting for our order of fries. I had never really had anything really unique spiritually happen before (in my first three months of being a Christian), but I can remember it like it was yesterday. I looked up and had almost an uncontrollable desire from God telling me to go stop a sixteen-wheeler that was just starting to pull out from the fuel pumps. I told Ken immediately, and he yelled, "What are you waiting for? Go, dude!" So I jumped from my seat ran through the crowd in the truck stop like I stole something. I ran out the double doors and into the pouring rain in pursuit of the moving semi. As it was approaching the access road, I jumped onto driver's side, grabbing the lift bar on the side and yelled, "Stop!" slapping the driver's window. The air brakes locked, and the door came open, almost knocking me to the ground. I wouldn't have blamed him if he had punched me right in the mouth looking back, but instead he looked at me with a perplexed look and said, "What are you doing!" I said, "You're not going to believe this, but I was eating fries with my friend in the restaurant, and I heard God tell me to stop your truck."

What happened next still amazes me to this day. The driver was not alone. He had a young woman in the passenger's seat. She was crying. He turned to me and said, "My girlfriend is Christian, and I love her very much. She told me that we can't be together anymore if I can't believe. I told her if God is real, why doesn't he ever show himself to me? Then you knocked on my window!" I don't know what happened after that day, but I do know this—a big, burly truck driver let his girlfriend and myself lead him to a new relationship with *Christ* that night. I have also heard others talk about a couple with a ministry for truck drivers that tell about how they started it when some crazy guy jumped on their truck one night in the rain.

#IKnowHim story submitted by Ken Bundy

Part 3

The Fear

Persecution

Despite knowing the responsibility carried by each believer to share the gospel and being fully aware of the battle that rages on over the name of Jesus, there is a large population of people who have had an encounter with Jesus who are still hesitant to tell the world that they know Him. The question we must ask ourselves is, "*Why?*" Why are we, the church, holding back when it comes to sharing our knowledge and experience that God is real, He is here, and He is good? Why is it seemingly difficult for us to even speak the name of Jesus without apprehension? Why is this hesitant group of believers often larger than the group of those willing to share what God has done in their lives?

Perhaps the most evident reason lies in the persecution of the church for proclaiming that they believe in God because they have seen Him move and felt His presence. They boldly confess that Jesus is Lord, knowing full well that their new lives in Christ are likely to be the cause of their physical deaths on earth, or worse, the deaths of their loved ones.

According to Open Doors USA, there are more than sixty-five countries in the world today that actively persecute Christians. A report from CNN[8] in cooperation with Open Doors USA highlighted that "Christian persecution reached a record high in 2015, a level akin to ethnic cleansing." In Morocco, for example, the .2 percent population of known Christians risk their lives daily by claiming the name of Jesus in the presence of their 99.8 percent Islamic community. These

---

[8] "Christian persecution reached record high in 2015," CNN, accessed January 1, 2017, http://www.cnn.com/2016/01/17/world/christian-persecution-2015/

four thousand believers in Morocco secretly attend house churches to encourage one another in their faith and to worship corporately. When they are caught, Christians are arrested or deported from their homeland. North Korea, also known for their widespread persecution of Christians send those who are caught to labor camps. These Christians face torture, imprisonment, and execution for simply claiming to know God. The country of Somalia is known to have only about two hundred Christians, who also meet in homes secretly. Conversion from Islam is forbidden, and Al-Shabab (a terrorist group that merged with Al Qaeda), immediately execute people claiming to know Jesus or anyone found with Christian literature within their possession.[9]

The world watched in paralyzing fear when ISIS released their video of their mass execution of Christians from around the world. Nothing could explain the stifling sickness in our stomachs as we got word of the video showcasing another brutal execution by ISIS on one believer, thrown into a cage and lit on fire to die a slow and torturous death. These terrorists, in the name of Islam, kidnap, rape, and enslave anyone who refuses to convert from Christianity. Anyone who is willing to stand and say that they know Jesus is a target for brutal persecution, often forced to watch their loved ones, their spouses, and their children brutally executed before their eyes, as they await their own death.

And yet—these believers remain steadfast. These followers of Jesus suffer atrocities no one should ever encounter, see, or hear … and at the end of it all, they stand firm in their faith, look persecution in the face by the power of one name and make terror and evil a footstool for their feet. These faithful brothers and sisters cling tight to that name above every name, the name of Jesus. When their time comes, and an enemy of the gospel is asking, "Do you know Him?" with fire in their bones and fervor in their eyes, and the saints who have gone before them cheering them on in their race, they answer with a resounding, "*I know Him.*" Their statement, like thunder, echoes through eternity. It ascends to heaven before the Father, and in victory He welcomes them home.

---

[9] "World Watch List," Open Doors, Accessed November 3, 2016, https://www.opendoorsusa.org/christian-persecution/world-watch-list/

Their confession descends to the pit of hell, echoing forever in the ears of the evil one, shaking his foundation as an eternal reminder that the resurrection has resurrected one more saint, and his time to dispel fear and evil to those who love God is about to come to a screeching halt.

While there are those who share their stories despite the persecution at their doors, there are some who choose to remain silent. The persecution is too great and the pain too much to risk for simply saying the name of Jesus. For the sake of their families, they remain silent. For the sake of their homes, they refuse to accept a Bible or any Christian literature. However, there are those beginning to stir in the shadows who know Him and have experienced His presence and the tug on their hearts to share what God has done for them, coming out of the hidden places inch by inch and into the light. As they wait for courage or for death, they pray silently for safety. They pray that if it comes time, they too may answer, "We must obey God rather than men" (Acts 5:29 ESV).

For those of us free to claim Christ without persecution, it is our privilege to pray for those in chains for knowing Him. The church collectively is called to "remember those in chains" and to pray for them earnestly. Let's come together to pray for their families, their freedom, and their faith to remain steadfast in the face of evil. Another way we can support our brothers and sisters is by writing letters to them, through an organization know as Voice of the Martyrs. They have a sign-up list through which you will receive names of people to pray for and where they are being held. This resource also shares stories of those being persecuted and does incredible things to get Bibles to those in persecuted countries. Likewise, Open Doors USA is a resource for anyone wanting more information on Christian persecution. Let us be inspired by their testimonies and encouraged to share what God has done for us all the more while we have the freedom to do so. For the sake of gospel, may not one second of our freedom be wasted.

Christian persecution isn't new to the world, as historically and biblically it has been around for thousands of years. In the Old Testament, it wasn't uncommon for prophets to be forced into hiding after delivering a message warning of the wrath of God to a ruler whose refusal to repent would lead their nation astray. These prophets would hide in caves until the ruler repented or God handled it. Yet, they remained steadfast to the mission to which God called them. In the New Testament we see the first man killed for his faith in the resurrected Christ, brutally murdered by stones at the hands of a devout Pharisee. Moments before his death, a recently assigned apostle named Stephen addressed his persecutors:

> You stiff-necked people, uncircumcised in heart and ears, you always resist the Holy Spirit. As your fathers did, so do you. Which of the prophets did your fathers not persecute? And they killed those who announced beforehand the coming of the Righteous One, whom you have now betrayed and murdered. (Acts 7:51–52 ESV)

With his feet firmly planted in the hope of the cross and filled with the Holy Spirit, Stephen had no fear of what man could do to him, what they would do to him.

> But they cried out with a loud voice and stopped their ears and rushed together at him. Then they cast him out of the city and stoned him. And the witnesses laid down their garments at the feet of a young man named Saul. And as they were stoning Stephen, he called out, "Lord Jesus, receive my spirit." And falling to his knees he cried out with a loud voice, "Lord, do not hold this sin against them." And when he had said this, he fell asleep. (Acts 7:57–60 ESV)

There is something uniquely powerful about someone facing certain death and yet having the resolve to genuinely pray for the persecutor. The very reason these people, our brothers and sisters, all over the world and in the past and present, are laying down their lives is so those who have yet to find Christ can see Him all the more clearly.

You see, early in the New Testament, persecution picked up speed because the government was trying to eliminate the rumors about Jesus;

the rumors that these people who loved Jesus were doing miraculous things through His power; the rumor that not even the cross could hold Jesus down, and that this King they mocked and murdered really was a valiant King who would overthrow their way of life by fulfilling the very law they had been so loyal to follow. The Pharisees and the Roman government worked together to stop this invisible force from gaining ground, to stop these followers of Jesus from speaking of any way to live life other than the one built on laws and traditions that bound the people to their rituals and sacrifices. The laws that kept them in line and under control.

However, there was one Pharisee, Gamiliel, who advised the angry mob to be weary of their violence against the new Christians. He had seen individuals come and claim heavenly authority, accumulate large followings, yet when they died, everything dispersed and went back to normal because there was no legitimate power behind the claims they made. For some reason, this highly esteemed Gamiliel discerned there was such a great deal of urgency within the government and the Pharisees to kill anyone following Christ, with little to no effectiveness in hindering the spread of the news of Christ, that he was moved to warn his peers:

> And he said to them, "Men of Israel, take care what you are about to do with these men. For before these days Theudas rose up, claiming to be somebody, and a number of men, about four hundred, joined him. He was killed, and all who followed him were dispersed and came to nothing. After him Judas the Galilean rose up in the days of the census and drew away some of the people after him. He too perished, and all who followed him were scattered. So in the present case I tell you, keep away from these men and let them alone, for if this plan or this undertaking is of man, it will fail; but if it is of God, you will not be able to overthrow them. You might even be found opposing God!" (Acts 5:35–39 ESV)

And here we are, over two thousand years later. Bearing witness to the same resurrection, the same power, the same name—the name that flipped the world upside down and introduced a kingdom economy of kindness, forgiveness, and faithfulness. This is the same name people are still going to war over today. The suffering is great, but the name of Jesus is greater still. There will never be any force that can come close to the unstoppable magnitude of the glory of God. There will never be a day when the last Christian is killed and evil triumphs. We can find peace and strength in the truth that just like our brothers and sisters who are fighting every day to stand firm in their faith, we too serve an unstoppable God. There is no last option for God, no last resort. Author and Bible teacher Beth Moore is quoted as saying, "A dead end means nothing to a God of resurrection."[10] There was no amount of persecution, pain, or suffering that would make Jesus surrender, and He freely gives us the resolve to keep fighting. The very reason we have stories to share about God in our midst is because He has never thrown in the towel, and neither have the multitudes who love Him. Generation after generation, He remains faithful while the angry mobs of the world get more violent toward the thought of a Savior. Those who despise the truth, the grim reality of their own need for a Savior, boast tolerance. Authentic Christianity is the most peaceful, love-advocating worldview, yet it is the most persecuted and least tolerated in the entire world. Why is it that a religion that threatens with murder is given the freedom to roam and conquer while Christians are forced to pray in secret, and any mention of the truth from scripture is cause for heated debate and restriction?

The message of the gospel cannot be stopped, and with our testimonies the hope of the cross will spread like wildfire across persecuted countries and far behind enemy lines. In his last letter, the apostle Paul writes, "Remember Jesus Christ, risen from the dead, the offspring of David, as preached in my gospel, for which I am suffering, bound with chains as a criminal. *But the word of God is not bound!*" (2

---

[10] "The Scandal of Election 2016," The LPM Blog, Accessed October 18, 2016, http://blog.lproof.org/2016/10/the-scandal-of-election-2016.html

Timothy 2:8–9 ESV; my emphasis). But praise be to God, because the Word of God is *not* bound! It is not bound now, and it will never be bound in the future. The word of the gospel is *right now* making its way through the underground churches, over national borders, and under walls of restriction, because people who know Him are taking it there.

I remember being at a retreat in high school, and as the speaker shared a little bit of his story with us, I was amazed at the things he had given up to follow Jesus. He grew up in a Muslim family, his dad being one of the most respected and devout Muslim leaders in a highly populated region. The young man, whose name is Afshin[11], shared that someone had given him a Bible, and he would secretly read it when he was just a child, fearful of what might happen if he was caught. The years went by, and because he was a young adult, he decided he was ready to begin a relationship with the God of the Bible. The day came when he knew he had to tell his father about his new faith, knowing what it would mean for his future. The future that had been financially secure, in which he would always have an excellent job and his father would be proud of him and his success, now hung in the balance with this one conversation. The young man was ready to risk it all because it was time to tell his father that *he knew Him.*

As I sat and listened to him tell his story, I just knew it was going to end up with his father being upset at first but supportive in the end, and even expected him to conclude with how his life in Christ resulted in the salvation of his father as well. But it didn't go that way. Afshin was kicked out of his house. He was disowned by his family and cut off from any future with them. He had no money and no home, but he had Jesus. Even more challenging to consider, perhaps, was that this did not happen across the globe, but about ten hours away from my hometown in Texas. Suffering for the name of Jesus is not rare, and telling the world that you know Him will always cost *something.* It may not be your house, your family, or even your future, but we are guaranteed there will be a price to pay.

---

[11] "About," Afshin Ziafat, Accessed October 9 2016, http://www.afshinziafat.com/about.php

Enemy Friendship

Sometimes the price that must be paid looks a lot like something we more than likely strive for every day rather than something painful or sacrificial. It isn't sacrificing our homes, careers, or families, but often it may be our friendships—not even necessarily with individuals but our friendship with a world that wants nothing to do with Jesus. What is it that holds us back from telling our neighbors why we have hope in Jesus? Is it our fear of seeming foolish? We believe others are not used to that kind of authenticity, and more than likely people around us will simply misunderstand that we are simply trying to share hope, and instead, would write us off as crazy religious fanatics. We fear that we would seem foolish to them if we really express our belief that God exists, and not only that He exists, but that He is on the move right now, leaving glimpses of Himself in our lives. First Corinthians 1:18 (NIV) prepares us for this when Paul writes, "For the message of the cross is foolishness to those who are perishing, but to us who are being saved it is the power of God."

You see, if we really know God, then we will have an overwhelming desire to share the power of the cross with people. We will possess this overwhelming urge to share the hope we have swelling inside us as we encounter people looking for hope. When we speak with someone about his or her distress, we will be thinking in the back of our minds about a time we were also desperate, and the way God displayed His saving power when He brought us out of that pit. In all our relationships, we are given opportunities to share what God has done for us, and how He has saved us. But how often do we silence that gentle, quiet voice of the Spirit, nudging us to share the hope that resides in the name of Jesus? We see the opportunity to speak light into darkness, hope to the hopeless, and peace to restless, and a lump rises in our throats as our stomachs drop along with our courage. If we were to mention God and His sovereignty, the power of the cross and the ultimate redemption story of Jesus, these people that we see day in and day out might never look at us the same. They might label us "Jesus freaks" or something worse. Perhaps they would label us unintelligent for believing that we were intelligently designed by a God who wants to be involved in our lives, rather than the result of a cosmic accident, alone and insignificant. And this world with which we so longingly want to be friends with simply won't accept it. They won't accept our light, the new freedom that we have in Christ, because they are blinded by the darkness in which they choose to dwell.

If everything we said in our conversations reflected an underlying belief that God created us and has a purpose for us it would undeniably alter our lives, our relationships, and our entire worldviews. There is no subtlety with the gospel of Christ. You either choose to allow its entrance into every part of your being (your heart, mind, and soul), or nothing at all. But following Jesus is not about fitting in; it's about crying out. It's about confessing our deep need for a Savior and watching Him show up in our lives as we await His return. It's about speaking up for the widow, the orphan, standing up for what is right even when our actions may be unpopular. The way we live and love in our communities is how the world will know we are His (John 15:35). If we didn't look the least bit different from the world around us, we would have to ask ourselves what Jesus we were really following.

Some people are hesitant to share what God has done for them because they know that the God of the Bible is not the god that the world is okay with. The god that the world is okay with is a god of complacency, tolerance for evil, and passivity. This is the god that a large number of people will claim to follow on Christmas and Easter, or even go to visit every Sunday in a church somewhere. Even some who claim to be evangelical preachers teach only about this god, the god who simply invites everyone to be okay with their own lives, lacking in conviction and power. The God of the Bible, however, is not powerless and cannot be contained within the walls of our churches. Yes, He meets us there, but He also goes with us when we walk out the doors, lives with us at home, and goes with us to work and school. He longs for a permanent residence in our hearts and is actively pursuing us, wanting us to experience a life abundant with Him.

But this is not the god that is most popular, because with the freedom that Christ brings comes the responsibility to bear His name. To live as a chosen daughter or son, freed from a life of sin, means to live differently than you did before you were set free. This responsibility of bearing His name looks like speaking the truth, whatever the cost. It means being willing to say the hard things to those we love who are trapped in the snares set up for them by the enemy, and to speak hope and victory into their lives by means of the cross. Being a follower of Jesus means boldly exposing that the popular way of thinking that "what's right for me may be wrong for you and what is wrong for you might be right for me and that's okay" is nothing but a lie. Being a follower of Jesus, bearing His name, and walking in His power means being willing to stand firm in the truth that there is only *one* way to happiness, life abundant, and eternity with Him and that way is Christ, no compromise. It means we are fiercely loyal in loving our people, but we love them to a greater degree when we are willing to tell them Jesus loves them just as they are, but He loves them too much to leave them there.

None of these oppositions are easy, especially when we spend our time cultivating a friendship with the world. But when we are more preoccupied with what other people think and walk on eggshells so we don't rock the boat with our faith, we also pay a price. In James 4:4 (NIV), we read, "You adulterous people, don't you know that friendship with the world means enmity against God? Therefore, anyone who chooses to be a friend of the world becomes an enemy of God."

Clearly, there is obvious tension between God and the world. Why is it that we cannot pursue both the world and God? John 3:16–17 (ESV) says, "For God so loved the world, that he gave his only Son, that whoever believes in him should not perish but have eternal life. For God did not send his Son into the world to condemn the world, but in order that the world might be saved through him." If God loves the world so much that He would send His only Son to die for the people in it, why does friendship with the world mean going against Him? God loves the world, the entire human race that inhabits the planet. He knows every single person and their dreams, their talents, and how many hairs are on their heads at any given moment. He knows their pain, their suffering, and their victories. God's love is fierce for those He created, whether they believe it or not, whether they believe in Him or not. But to be a friend of the world in the context of James 4:4 is not meaning simply to be friends with those in the world, but to pursue an alignment with a lifestyle that opposes God.

The reason God sent His Son to die on the cross was to save the world. A world that needs saving is a world that is hurting. A world that needs saving is a world that is completely overwhelmed with darkness, choosing to abide in things that will pass away rather than the abundant life following God guarantees. Friendship with the world means choosing to deny the need for a Savior, thus rejecting the ultimate sacrifice paid by the brutal murder Jesus endured on the cross. Living a life pursuing friendship with the world signifies living a carnal lifestyle; it is all about appeasing the flesh in the moment—living for today and not caring about tomorrow. Friendship with the world means enmity with God because it alters our focus from His glory and His will for our lives to our own. God's desire is for the world to be saved, so when we choose to keep our love for Him and His Word silent and live a life that blends in with the sin-trapped world around us, we are hindering the ultimate goal of God: we are delaying others from being saved. If we are silent about the salvation and the light residing in us, how are our friends, family, and neighbors going to know there is a way to live life in the abundance that God intends for us?

There is a popular C. S. Lewis quote I have never been able to forget. In his book, *The Weight of Glory*, Lewis writes:

> It would seem that Our Lord finds our desires not too strong, but too weak. We are half-hearted creatures, fooling about with

drink and sex and ambition when infinite joy is offered us, like an ignorant child who wants to go on making mud pies in a slum because he cannot imagine what is meant by the offer of a holiday at the sea. We are far too easily pleased.[12]

Friendship with the world means sacrificing a life far more incredible than we could imagine for the temporary pleasure of this passing world. Worldly friendship lives with the perspective that all that matters is happiness in the moment, rather than joy eternal and prioritizing what matters most. If we find ourselves working more strenuously to live a life that is approved by a worldly standard than a life that is approved by God, we have missed the point of following Jesus and are residing in a fortress of deception built on sand.

If we have been set free by Christ, redeemed by His love, and restored by His unconditional grace, it is our responsibility (and our joy!) to share what He has done for us so others who are still in bondage can know that there is a way out. The people around us are hurting and are looking for new options, or alternative routes to the current lives they are living. Some of them have been chained to addiction for years, and think it is too late. They are believing the lie that God's grace has run out, and there is no way they can change. Imagine what it would mean for them to hear that someone like them, either down their street or even on the other side of the world who had been chained to addiction for years, without hope of redemption or restoration, was completely set free when they gave their life to Christ. When they said *yes* to Jesus and allowed Him to enter in and He created something completely new. In 2 Corinthians 5:17 (NIV), the author writes. "Therefore, if anyone is in Christ, the new creation has come: The old has gone, the new is here!"

To anyone who has ever wanted to start over, to be made completely new, there is a way for that to happen. For the forty-year-old woman who feels stuck in her circumstances—there is a way for God to create something new. For the young man, who like the prodigal son (Luke 15) is ready to return home after a life of resisting God, there is a way to begin a new life, completely restored by the blood of the Lamb. When

---

[12] C.S. Lewis, *The Weight of Glory,* (New York, New York, Harper Collins, 1949) 26

we confess that we need a Savior and make Jesus the reigning Lord of our lives, in that same moment we are free to walk confidently before God, blameless.

If we have been given new life, we have an incredible story to tell. If we have been set free from sin and shame, and carried through trial after trial, it is our responsibility to let others know that it is possible for them too. Yes, the world will be watching. But they will also be listening. There will always be a price to pay for knowing Jesus, but the price for not knowing Him is vastly more costly. So what if people think we are strange for saying the name of Jesus in public? In the end, what do people's opinions of us mean? If we as believers are obedient to what God is asking us to do, step by step, we will deny the world a friendship that would have ultimately led to destruction. Instead, we will love others fiercely by telling the truth about what God has done for us and wants to do for them.

When I was in high school, my youth group spent a couple of days serving in a city about an hour away from my hometown. While part of this experience was spent studying the Bible and in discipleship, another aspect of this retreat was to step out of our comfort zones by sharing the gospel on the streets. This is by far one of the least popular things to do in our culture today. People want privacy. We seek isolation when in crowds by avoiding eye contact and making our phones seem more relevant than the person standing two feet away in order to avoid conversation. People generally do not want to hear about the name of Jesus in public settings, especially in any place other than a church they voluntarily walk into. Just the name of Jesus makes people uncomfortable. It's as if some people assume judgment and hypocrisy will invade the air every time someone brings Him up. But that's not how the name of Jesus works. The name of Jesus makes people uncomfortable because it is the name above every name, and it is at His name that every knee will bow. When two or more gather in the name of Jesus (Matthew 18:20), the atmosphere changes because the Spirit of God begins to move. We feel the tension as our flesh is confronted with a force far superior, beckoning us to a new life free from our comfortable pits of bondage. When the name of Jesus is spoken, mountains begin to move, hard hearts are softened, and we are confronted with eternity.

Nonetheless, this was part of our agenda while on the retreat as a sort of training, and we selected a spot where our group would split up and hold up large white banners with the name of Jesus in bright, bold, red letters printed on it. Subtle, right? After a few hours, a car pulled up next to the youth pastor, and I looked over and saw an intense conversation going on between him and the woman in the car. I later found out that she and her husband had found drugs in their son's room, and in a moment of desperation, they got on their knees on the floor by his bed and cried out to God. They were brokenhearted and knew their son had been making bad decisions for a while. Tension had been building in their home, and everything seemed to be falling apart. They asked God to send an army of angels after their son, so that he could come face-to-face with Jesus. The woman told our youth minister that her son worked in the tall building down the street from where our groups were stationed, and in about fifteen minutes, he would drive past all of our banners, see the large group of young believers, and come face-to-face with the name of Jesus on his way to work.

As students, we had been nervous and apprehensive about this street ministry for obvious reasons but decided to boldly walk together to tell the world that we knew Him. I can't help but think about what would have happened if our group decided it was too much of a risk, would be too uncomfortable, or would have been much too awkward. God divinely orchestrated us to be on that street, in that large city, that day, to act as an army, an army carrying the name of Jesus, banner lifted high, so *one* young man whose mother was desperately praying, would remember to whom he belonged—that he would see another way out of the mess he was in and maybe even take it.

Our decisions make eternal differences. Whether we choose to share what God has done for us or not, the world will keep spinning until one day, it will stop. We are given the opportunity to choose whether we will be for God or against Him until our last breath, or until the very moment He comes back. In the meantime, it is up to us to determine if we are willing to be uncomfortable for the sake of sharing hope and freedom with our neighbors, our friends, and our co-workers. If we pursue friendship with the world rather than loyalty to God, we will become a hindrance to the very saving of the world we were trying to appease.

The Cross Is Heavy

One thing that is unique about those who forsake friendship with the world to tell their stories is that they have made a conscious decision to throw off any personal hindrances that might stop them from publicly carrying the cross. They have understood the responsibility that accompanies freedom in Christ. When bearing the name of Jesus, there is a closely knit, intimate tension that is rooted in the power behind the name. It is because of this tension that many people decide to continue blending in, choosing to keep what God has done in their lives their best-kept secret.

You see, when we carry the name of Jesus, there is incredible liberty that is immediately gifted to us, completely undeserved and unearned. We are given the gift of starting over, saying no to bondage, shame, and guilt as we say yes to a life empowered by the Spirit. But we are also immediately given a heavy responsibility. If we choose to carry the name of Jesus, we are committing to do all we can to represent Him well. If we choose to commit, this responsibility must seep into every single area of our lives, altering the way we do life on every level. When we say that God has set us free, saved us, and redeemed us, we are acknowledging that we are in need a Savior. We are offering our stories and our hearts to be laid completely bare for the world to see. When we bear the name of Jesus, we are presented with the incredible opportunity to lay our pasts out in the light, to walk in a new life honoring God and completely rely on Him to supply the words we need at just the moment we need them. To say yes to these opportunities means we are saying yes to God, using whatever He desires in our lives in an effort to honor the name of Jesus.

As great as this sounds, in reality all these opportunities are extremely costly and more often than not, quite painful for the story teller. These responsibilities, these opportunities, are some of the biggest hindrances to people sharing what God has done in their lives because of what it means for their lives presently. Everyone has a past, and every single past is unique to the individual. But in sharing that Jesus has saved us, we admit that we were in dire need of a Savior. This looks different for everyone, but in every circumstance of a sinner being saved, there had to be sin involved. Likewise, I have yet to meet one person who has been proud of his or her sin, of the darkness he or she was brought out of by Christ. When we share our stories, we are sharing our vulnerable pasts, our hearts when they were broken, and our dirty rags for the world to see.

If we share who we used to be, we run the risk of people seeing us that way forever. This is exactly how our enemy wants us to feel. If we share our sin, we might be given a red letter describing that sin from which we were saved labeling us as such until the day we die. I have a friend who once described feeling as if she wore a scarlet D after going through a divorce. I've since heard many more women describe that exact feeling, which reveals just how common this strategy is utilized by the deceiver. What the enemy doesn't want us to remember is what really happens when we confess that sin; we are given a new label to wear forever, one that reads, "Redeemed, forgiven, and free." First John 1:9 (ESV) says, "If we confess our sins, he is faithful and just to forgive us our sins and to cleanse us from all unrighteousness." *He* is faithful and just. And *He* is all that matters. If we confess our sins to God, He will absolutely forgive us. This means that despite whatever anyone else may think when we share our testimonies, regardless of what kind of mess they start with, our stories end in victory. Our stories end in redemption. Our stories include a blameless future because the blood of the Lamb has covered all our sin, and that is what is important for people to hear.

If the highlight of our pasts is not what we have done but what has been done to us, Satan is sure to create anxiety and fear over what it means to share that part of our lives as well. Retelling the moments that broke our hearts, wounded our bodies and minds, and left us with deep scars as a remembrance of what we have survived is not only intimidating, but it can also create an atmosphere of distress for us, as if we were having to sort through all the emotions of that hardship for the first time. The battle here is internal. Those on the outside do not see us as weak regarding our circumstances but only as an incredibly strong survivor despite them. But on the inside, it is as if it happened yesterday, and the road ahead can appear just as dark as the night before. In retelling our painful pasts, we are given the opportunity to remind ourselves, the world, and the enemy that even in the midst of unimaginable heartbreak, we still belong to God. We remind ourselves especially that God works out everything for the good of those who love Him (Romans 8:28), and by His power, we can move forward, taking each step one at a time by simply putting one foot in front of the other in obedience to what He is asking of us. In Philippians 3:13–14 (ESV) we read, "But one thing I do: forgetting what lies behind and straining forward to what lies ahead, I press on toward the goal for the prize of the upward call of God in Christ Jesus." When we share what God has done for us, even when it hurts, we are choosing to press on. We do not walk forward blindly, but He goes with us and keeps our eyes focused on what lies ahead. Every day that we press on is one more day Satan has lost hold of us, and we are free to run our race once again.

Sharing our stories often means giving whoever we share it with (whether that be a friend, a coworker, a neighbor, or even a family member) exactly what they could use to hurt us in some way. This is a legitimate fear of many people resistant to share what God has done for them, and it is understandable. However, if we are choosing to bear the name of Jesus, we must also understand that if we offer up our vulnerable selves to God for Him to use for His purpose, He can do something astounding with our testimonies, something that we could not even in our wildest dreams do for ourselves. In Isaiah 43:18–19 (ESV), the prophet writes,

> Remember not the former things, nor consider the things of old. Behold, I am doing a new thing; now it

springs forth, do you not perceive it? I will make a way
in the wilderness and rivers in the desert.

God can do incredibly wonderful things in our lives with what
we have experienced if we are only brave enough to share it. There
is another hindrance here, though, that must be addressed. If we are
publicly proclaiming we have been set free and God has done something
incredible and new, those who hear our stories will have something of
a new standard to which they uphold our lives. If we say we have fallen
in love with Jesus and He has saved us, then even the unbelieving world
expects us to live in such a way that reflects our new lives in Christ.
This in itself is not a bad thing, but the hindrance is rooted in the fear
that the people who are watching and waiting to see how we live out
our new lives are actually watching and waiting for us to *fail*. We fear
they are waiting for us to return to living in a manner that they are
used to, or the very manner in which they live, if they have not been
freed themselves.

However, those who are waiting and watching for believers to fail
have their eyes on the wrong individual. Those who follow Jesus do not
become perfect after they confess their sins and believe that Christ was
raised. Their lives are altered, both here and for eternity, but they still
must wage war daily with the flesh in which they reside while on earth.
People who have decided to follow Jesus do so because they know in
the depths of their souls that He is the only one who *will never fail*.
People who follow Jesus are inevitably going to mess up, because they
are *people*. There is only one God, and neither we nor the people who
seem to be rooting for us to fail are Him. What matters most is how we,
as believers, respond when we do fall short. There is almost no greater
testimony of what God has done for us than that of how we behave
when we know we have messed up, and in humility come before God
and our peers, claiming His strength in our weakness. Titus 2:7–8
(ESV) gives us some direction on how to respond in these matters:
"Show yourself in all respects to be a model of good works, and in
your teaching show integrity, dignity, and sound speech that cannot be

condemned, so that an opponent may be put to shame, having nothing evil to say about us." Likewise, in 2 Corinthians 6:3 (ESV) we read, "We put no obstacle in anyone's way, so that no fault may be found with our ministry." No matter how we fail, if we bear the name of Jesus, we must continually strive for forgiveness and grace, constantly pointing to the One who paid for it all. We must strive to live lives that are holy and pleasing to God so that as believers, when others are watching us and how we respond, we only show them *more* of the gospel and what God has done and *is continually* doing for us.

Anytime we step out in faith to share what God has done for us, people will undoubtedly begin to look at our lives and watch how we live out this faith we say has changed our lives, and most of the time with good reason and intention. If we have been saved by Christ, we are to live a life set apart. We are *supposed* to live like we are new, if in fact Christ has made us new. Why would someone who claims to have been freed from addiction return to it the very next day, with no remorse or change of heart? If we have been set free from Christ, then we have truly been freed and our lives and our testimonies are meant to be a beacon of light and hope for weary souls looking for relief. In his gospel, Matthew records Jesus saying, "You are the light of the world. A city set on a hill cannot be hidden. Nor do people light a lamp and put it under a basket, but on a stand, and it gives light to all in the house. In the same way, let your light shine before others, so that they may see your good works and give glory to your Father who is in heaven" (Matthew 5:14–16 ESV). If we have been given the light of Christ, and our dark hearts brought out in to the light, our lives should shine brighter than those who don't have the light of Christ. This is definitely not saying that our lives should be easier by any means (in fact, in most cases it seems to be quite the opposite) but that they should reflect the freedom and the hope and the power that resides in us.

One of my favorite illustrations of the importance of doing the work to set our lives apart from the world comes from Joshua 3. Joshua has just been put in command of the Israelites as Moses instructed, and they have come to the Jordan River, where they must cross carrying the ark of the covenant to enter the Promised Land. God told Joshua He would provide a way for them to get across by means of a supernatural miracle. God was going to prohibit the Jordan from flowing, and the feet of the Israelites would cross the Jordan on dry ground. But before they crossed the Jordan, Joshua, in this moment in history, speaks to God's chosen people and instructs them, "Then Joshua said to the people, 'Consecrate yourselves, for tomorrow the Lord will do wonders among you'" (Joshua 3:5 ESV). Other translations write that the Israelites were instructed to "sanctify" themselves before crossing the Jordan. Either way it is a powerful example of our responsibility to live our lives like we truly have been redeemed because we have been redeemed indeed.

I also think it is interesting that Joshua would make the distinct connection of consecration *today* in preparation for what the Lord would do *tomorrow*. It is so important for us to consecrate ourselves, stay humble, and remember what God has done for us, reflecting the magnitude of what Jesus did for us, so we can make room in our hearts and our lives for God to move mightily. In today's world, it is so easy to let our hearts become clustered with sin and pride, getting so caught up in temporary things that we forget to live set apart, failing to remember what we have been brought out of and become so distracted by pleasing others that we miss out on preparing our hearts for the incredible wonders that God wants to do in our futures. If we want to make room for God to do big wonders, we need to clean house and get rid of the sin that beckons us back to bondage.

When we tell others that we have had an experience with God, we are vulnerably sharing a past redeemed but also committing to a future redeemed. We are to walk boldly with the confidence that God will honor those who say no to fear and will empower us to stand firm in the freedom and restoration God brings. Redemption storytellers bravely walk in obedience, one foot in front of the other, accepting the weight of responsibility that accompanies the freedom of a life in Christ. While it is a responsibility to live a life worthy of representing the name of Jesus, it is nothing short of a privilege to speak of what God has done, no matter the cost. My prayer for us is that when we are faced with fear or anxiety of any sort that could be a hindrance to sharing our stories, we would pray for God's perspective. And in doing so, my hope is that we would determine to count any sacrifice an honor to suffer for the name of Christ (Acts 5:41).

We were so young. Both barely twenty, my husband and I had been married only a few months when God began prompting us to take a life-altering trip to the city of Dubai. One spring evening, we listened intently as a mentor-friend of ours described her upcoming short-term mission trip to Dubai. God had been prompting her to make travel arrangements to Dubai to search out a specific person who was trapped in the bondage of human trafficking, more specifically, in sexual slavery. God revealed to our friend that someone in Dubai had been crying out to Him to be rescued. Though God had not revealed the name of the captive our friend was to find, she was confident He would help her identify this enslaved person once she arrived in the city, and He would provide the way to freedom.

As our friend spoke, my eyes were fixed on my husband's facial expression as he marveled at God's intricate redemptive work unfurling. Though genuinely moved at what I could hear the Lord was doing in the life of our friend, I was fearful the invitation had just been extended to us as well. And it turned out I was right. A moment later, the invitation hung in the air: "...and I am looking for a small team to go with me."

Deep fears coursed through my mind, and my heart flooded with whispers of doubt and thoughts of my own weakness. I wanted my heart to be willing, but I was terrified to take the risk. A city and culture foreign to our experience, twenty-first-century slaves in bondage ... could God really use us to make a difference? Yet reaching from the throne of heaven into our hearts that night was the wonderful mystery of God calling His people to sacrifice self, becoming available ambassadors in His rescue plan for another of His children.

After much consideration and prayer, our answer together became a faith-filled yes, and the many details spun into action as we had only a couple of months until our departure. We needed to request time off work, pray and study, finalize travel details, and faced the overwhelming task of raising one-third of my husband's gross annual income for that year to cover necessary trip expenses. It is utterly laughable to consider the impossibility of the circumstances we faced, but God didn't seem to mind our concerns or the humble dollar amount attached to our newlywed bank account. God had our willingness, so He caused every door necessary to His purpose to be opened by His power alone. From the moment we said yes to the adventure He was preparing, our fears faded as we watched Him make the path straight before us.

After weeks of watching God move countless mountains to make our venture possible, we purchased the only two remaining seats on the flight our friend had booked weeks before, and our team of three soared to Dubai on the wind.

As in any large city in the world, secrets abound behind the lure of attractive busyness and beauty. In our first days in Dubai, we learned this firsthand as we prayed and walked city streets. We spoke with locals about their city and its happenings and begged God to prepare us as we sought out the one(s) He sent us to find. We napped during the heat of day, then ventured out each night onto the street in front of our hotel as it bustled with illegal activity. Girls from nations around the world lined the street just near our hotel. Cash was continually exchanged through quick car window transactions as the girls released their most recent earnings to fierce-eyed bosses; the sight was devastatingly overwhelming. Stunned by the vast number of women prostituting in this location, I began to wonder how God would point out who we were meant to find.

The first two nights we made attempts to communicate with several women but struggled through language barriers unsuccessfully. We were giving our every ounce of availability to the purpose to which we were called; our hearts were willing, but our physical energy and hopes of helping were beginning to faint in the desert heat, so again we cried out for God's help.

On the third night, our team of three returned to the street weary in every way, yet armed with hope in God. Hours came and went, praying and waiting. Then at the most unexpected moment, we lifted our eyes, and there they stood: two treasures in the desert night. As in a movie scene, people all around us became a blur to our eyes, while these two girls stood out to us as diamonds reflecting sunlight. Their gaze caught ours and hung in the air on an invisible line, with what felt like the weight of the world dangling between. We stepped forward along shadowy sidewalk squares in their direction, into exactly what the Lord had planned for us to find.

That night, we listened to our new friends' stories, learned their real names, and worked together to devise a plan to help them regain freedom. The girls relayed to us the deception they had endured, as months before they were tricked into moving to Dubai from their home country under the assumption they would be given jobs as housekeepers or other legitimate employment opportunities. They were promised these jobs would allow them to make a much better living than those available to them in their home country, providing them the opportunity to send money back to their families regularly. Upon arrival in Dubai, the girls' passports and freedom were stolen. Shattered at their new reality, they were forced by their captors into prostitution until they were able to attain the large sum of money required to retrieve their passports. Hopes of a better life were crushed in the greedy fists of their captors, and the shame of being deceived into a life of prostitution was immeasurably painful.

They expressed their belief in Jesus Christ and told of their desperate prayers to God to rescue them from slavery. As we listened to one another's stories regarding the months prior to meeting, we pieced together the timeline of their first prayers for God's rescuing was perfectly consistent with our mentor-friend's initial prompting to go to Dubai and search them out!

In the days following our initial meeting, we continued to get to know our newfound friends, and God provided a way for our team to meet with their boss, purchasing back the girls' passports to regain their freedom. We looked on amazed as their passports were returned into their hands and tearfully rejoiced as they held them close and kissed the pages. God had restored these girls to freedom, and through their story, their boss was moved to quit this unjust work and find legitimate employment as well! God displayed the splendor of His might before our eyes as we watched the captives set free and the heart of a captor softened toward Him.

Through this adventure, we have seen that nothing in all the earth can keep us from the love of God. Scripture tells us emphatically that no trouble or calamity, no persecution, not even the powers of hell can separate us from God's love. God makes Himself known, that we may know Him. He has gone to greatest measure, the sacrifice of His only Son, that we may each know the reality of His presence with us, and the goodness of His love. He seeks out the lost, the lonely, the hurting, the persecuted to redeem them to Himself, and He will stop at nothing to make His love known to you.

Do you know Him?

#IKnowHim story submitted by Sydney Clark

Part 4

The Charge

We Are the Storytellers

#IKnowHim is a call to action. It is a charge to those who have experienced God to go to war on darkness by saying no to fear and boldly sharing their stories. This charge is not to draw attention to the storyteller but to the author of the story—to proclaim God's goodness to all people and to remind Satan that he is not the one who writes our stories. God has already written the end to Satan's story, and our testimonies remind him that his time here is short. God is on the move, and with every second that passes, every wonder and miracle passed on from one generation to the next, every story of every person set free by Christ that travels from one person to the next, the enemy grows weaker and weaker, closer still to his final defeat.

In Revelation 12:11–12 (NIV) we see both of these forces (our testimonies and the enemy) in action:

> And they have conquered him by the blood of the Lamb and by the word of their testimony, for they loved not their lives even unto death. Therefore, rejoice, O heavens and you who dwell in them! But woe to you, O earth and sea, for the devil has come down to you in great wrath, because he knows that his time is short!

Our debt was paid by the blood of the Lamb, and Satan cannot stand it. Satan's aim is to deceive as many people as he can about who Jesus really is and their need for Him. Satan's ultimate goal is to prevent as many people as he can from establishing a relationship with God that will allow them to enter the gates of heaven, and he will accomplish this by whatever means necessary.

While evidence of God on the move is abundant, so is the work of the devil. He knows his time is coming to an end, so he toils all the more to keep those who believe silent while he wreaks havoc on the earth. The light that we carry when we bear the name of Jesus has the ability to drive out any darkness that we encounter. When we share the gospel of Christ by vulnerably sharing our stories, we add yet another torch to the flame of the body of Christ. Collectively, the flames of the church grow brighter as we share what God has done in our lives, and the devil *trembles.* The flame grows stronger each time someone boldly faces the darkness, and even in the midst of immense turmoil, they proclaim that God is real, God is here, and He is good; and the enemy *flees.* Every time a believer uses his or her testimony to encourage those who follow Jesus and to inspire those who have not yet believed to simply lift up their eyes and see God moving, Satan's sure defeat is closer still.

In his book *The Pursuit of God*, author A. W. Tozer writes, "If my fire is not large it is yet real, and there may be those who can light their candle at its flame."[13] This is the ultimate goal of living a life for Jesus: that by our testimonies others might pursue Christ and salvation, ultimately bringing glory to Him whom all glory is due. The purpose of telling stories about God on the move is to bring glory to God for doing incredible things in our lives despite our weaknesses. Throughout scripture God encourages us to tell of the wonders He has done for us—to tell our families, our cities, our friends, everyone who hasn't yet heard how He moved on our behalf to make His glory known.

Of this the psalmist writes, "I will tell of your name to my brothers; in the midst of the congregation I will praise you" (Psalm 22:22 ESV). We tell our brothers and sisters the power Jesus has displayed in our lives to encourage them to look for it in their lives as well. We sing songs about God doing incredible things to inspire the church to keep their eyes lifted to Christ who is the mountain mover, the chain breaker, and

---

[13] A. W. Tozer, *The Pursuit of God,* (Harrisburg, PA., Christian Publications, Inc., 1948), Introduction

the freedom fighter. Likewise in Psalm 66:16 (ESV) we read, "Come and hear, all you who fear God, and I will tell what he has done for my soul." Everyone loves inspiring stories, those that end happily, but think for a moment about those stories that do not end well. Now imagine someone who loves Jesus more than anything, sharing a story of unimaginable heartbreak and going on to say, "Now let me tell you what God has done for my soul through it *all*." If someone can survive being cast down in ultimate despair and stand to say that God is *still* good, there is obvious power in their anchor of hope.

What this can mean to someone in the trenches of heartache, stuck in the dire mess of their lives, is that there is One who moves on behalf of the hurting. There is One who refuses to sit idly by and watch those He loves suffer. It does not mean our circumstances will change overnight or maybe even ever, but it *does* mean that He moves in power to do incredible things for our souls that will never pass away.

A powerful example of this is found in the book of Daniel. After throwing three of his best men into a furnace for refusing to bow down to the idol he constructed, King Nebuchadnezzar was shocked to see the men walking around in the flames, unbound and unharmed. Perhaps even more shocking was that there appeared to be a fourth man with them, who onlookers declared was "like a son of the gods." The king ordered the men to be delivered out of the furnace, and after seeing that not one hair had been burnt, Nebuchadnezzar proclaimed, "There is no other God who is able to rescue in this way" (Daniel 3:29 ESV). Soon thereafter, the king made another proclamation to the people: "It has seemed good to me to show the signs and wonders that the Most High God has done for me. How great are his signs, how mighty his wonders!" (Daniel 4:2–3 ESV).

The king had an incredible encounter with God and chose to share what He had done in his midst. Unfortunately, later in his life Nebuchadnezzar chose to forget the wonders of God that he witnessed with his own eyes and quit telling his story. But by God's sovereignty, there were many in the audience who heard Nebuchadnezzar tell of God's presence and His goodness that day, and that impact was *eternal*. Our stories do not stop after we experience God once. We are frail, weak, sinners who continually need God to step in and save us, day after day.

In Acts 17:24–27 (NIV), scripture beautifully explains how His goodness is actually near to those seeking Him, all along their journeys:

> The God who made the world and everything in it is the Lord of heaven and earth and does not live in temples built by human hands. And he is not served by human hands, as if he needed anything. Rather, he himself gives everyone life and breath and everything else. From one man he made all the nations, that they should inhabit the whole earth; and he marked out their appointed times in history and the boundaries of their lands. God did this so that they would seek him and perhaps reach out for him and find him, though he is not far from any one of us.

It is not just one story we have to tell, but countless stories of God being evident in our lives when He is present and near to us in times of trial. We tell our stories as they happen but also recount what God has done in our lives so we don't forget what we have been set free from, and the ultimate redemption story. When we are looking for stories to share, God will move mightily in our lives giving us stories to tell of His goodness, so that others might desire to know Him too. Similarly, the author of Hebrews 4:16 (NIV) writes of the goodness found in His grace to us: "Let us then approach God's throne of grace with confidence, so that we may receive mercy and find grace to help us in our time of need."

Praise God that our stories are not dependent on our abilities to emerge from the pit and stay free by our own strength. Regardless of whether we fail the very next day and need to repent all over, we hold fast to grace but stand firm in truth because there is one thing we do know as storytellers of God: we have seen God. We have seen Him move our hearts out of darkness and into the light. We have seen what Jesus did on the cross to atone for our sins and make a way for us to be with God forever. We have seen Him step in and do wonders in our lives.

The apostle John records an instance in which we see this illustrated beautifully:

> So for the second time they called the man who had been blind and said to him, "Give glory to God. We know that this man is a sinner." He answered, "Whether he is a sinner I do not know. One thing I do know, that though I was blind, now I see." (John 9:24–25 ESV)

All that mattered to the blind man was that he had an encounter with Jesus, and his whole life changed for the better in an instant. At this point in Jesus's ministry, His popularity was waning and the future bleak. His death was around the corner, and those who followed Him were becoming scarce. It wasn't popular for the blind man to tell the world that he knew Him, but he knew that he couldn't deny his encounter with Jesus.

When we have an experience with God, nothing else compares to what He has done for us. It is these stories of Jesus standing with us in the fire, healing our hearts, and making Himself known to us that make others want to know *Him.* This is why we say no to fear. This is why we say no to the enemy. This is why we say yes to sharing that we know Him.

It is for those who have already believed and those yet to believe that we answer the call to share our stories. It is because God has done everything for us, and we should offer our lives back to Him to be used for whatever He requires to accomplish the goal of saving the world (as He tells us in John 3:16–17). This is applicable to every person who has chosen to follow Jesus, every person who has already accepted the gift of grace offered to us by God through the cross. As James explains in Revelation 14:12 (NIV), "This calls for patient endurance on the part of the people of God who keep his commands and remain faithful to Jesus." And while the struggle to carry the cross is very real, so is the faith that we have in Jesus to give us the strength to do exactly what He asks.

One night as I was listening to worship music after a long day, I felt God begin to move my heart to meditate on what it was He was asking of me. I felt like I had given everything I possibly could offer. And yet, here I was, having an encounter with Christ as He gently nudged my heart to be a little more vulnerable—to step out into deeper water and share what He was doing in my life yet again, because what He had already done for me, He longed to do for someone else.

This is something He continues to do in my life to this day. He reminds me of the strength He offers to carry on, to boldly speak the name of Jesus even when I am fearful or anxious. God is constantly reminding me of the task in front of me and the prize that lies ahead. The prize is eternal salvation, and when I can share the good news of the gospel with someone else as I tell my story, it's like Satan is defeated all over again. But it never gets easier to do so without some supernatural shoving.

When I feel like I have absolutely *nothing* left to give, He gently pushes me to give a little more. Because honestly, we can almost always do a little more, if not a great deal more if we really wanted to. When God asks something really big and scary of us, such as a career change or even a book like this or a big dream, it is really easy to let fear or anxiety become such a heavy burden that it disillusions us to believe we can't possibly lift anything else up as an offering to Him. This is just what the enemy wants us to believe. The truth is that because we have the Holy Spirit in us, we have absolutely everything to give and absolutely nothing less will do. We have an extremely powerful resource that will never run dry.

When we use what we think is our last step to serve Him, He gives us the power to take another. And another, and another … all the way until His kingdom comes in fullness. He asks this of us because the time we have here is too short and the risk far too great for us not to give everything.

Every time I begin to do something He is asking of me, I ask that the Holy Spirit puts a fire in my bones that gives me a little *more*. A little more energy, a little more wisdom, a little more inspiration, a little more *grace*. Out of this intimate moment with God, I began to pray from another perspective. I began fully expecting God to take this offering of ours (the words of our testimonies) and make it into everything He desires, and nothing less. This is incredibly powerful (and a little scary) to meditate on. The God of the universe has nothing but love for us, and His desire is for everyone to *know Him*. First Timothy 2:3–4 (ESV) tells us, "This is good, and it is pleasing in the sight of God our Savior, who desires all people to be saved and to come to the knowledge of the truth."

The thought that He could take what we are offering (our time, hearts, vulnerability, and words) and make it into something that spreads for the glory of His name is nothing short of amazing. My prayer is that God uses #IKnowHim to further His kingdom to let someone out there know that He is *here*, He is *real*, and He is *good*. And those of us on the fence about boldly sharing what He has done for us should never forget that if we have a relationship with Christ, we are promised that the Spirit lives in us (2 Timothy 1:14, Romans 8:11). We have everything to give. And nothing less.

For Such a Time as This

There is one particular story from the Old Testament that has always captivated me. The biblical account is about a young girl who went by the name of Esther. Orphaned at a young age, she was brought up by her Jewish uncle, Mordecai. They lived in Susa, where they were ruled by King Ahasuerus. When Esther was just a young woman, still under the care of Mordecai, the king gave a feast for all the people of Susa, small and great alike. The king demanded that his wife, Queen Vashti, be brought out at the end of the feast "in order to show the peoples and the princes her beauty, for she was lovely to look at" (Esther 1:11 ESV). The queen, understandably, did not want to be delivered to the king simply so a bunch of drunken men could stare at her. Boldly, she refused the king's order.

Obviously, this did not make the king look good in front of his guests. In order to overcome the subordination and humiliation, his advisor suggested that he make an example out of her. The king decreed that he would take her royalty away from her and would choose a new queen. And just like that, the king was on the hunt. He appointed officers to gather all the young, beautiful virgins in Susa to be brought under the custody of Hegai, the king's eunuch who was in charge of the women (Esther 2:3). As a result of the decree, young Esther was also taken into custody. Scripture tells us that she quickly won the favor of Hegai, and her beauty advanced her to the top seven in running for the position of the queen. The plot then begins to thicken as we learn that Esther had kept her Jewish heritage a secret, because Mordecai had instructed her to do so for her safety. Every day Mordecai, knowing what was at risk if they learned of her Jewish background, "walked in front of the court of the harem to learn how Esther was and what was happening to her" (Esther 2:11 ESV).

After a year of preparation, the time came for each of the women to meet the king. Each woman would leave their harem, go in to be with the king for one night, and then be moved to a new harem, the house for the concubines. They would not see the king again, unless "he delighted in her and she was summoned by name" (Esther 2:14 ESV). We see that when it was Esther's turn to meet the king, God had given her favor and had a new future in store for her:

> Now Esther was winning favor in the eyes of all who saw her. And when Esther was taken to King Ahasuerus, into his royal palace, in the tenth month, which is the month of Tebeth, in the seventh year of his reign, the king loved Esther more than all the women, and she won grace and favor in his sight more than all the virgins, so that he set the royal crown on her head and made her queen instead of Vashti. (Esther 2:15–17 ESV)

This young girl, once orphaned, was now a queen. It sounds like the perfect fairy tale, for a moment. Her faithful uncle Mordecai remained at the gates every day to keep watch over the daughter he had adopted and raised as his own. One day while at the gates, he overheard two of the king's officers scheming to kill the king. Mordecai immediately got the news to Esther, who told the king in the name of Mordecai, and the incident was documented.

After a while, another man named Haman was promoted by the king, and all were commanded to bow down and pay their respects to Haman. But Mordecai, who bowed down only to God, refused. In his fury, Haman devised a plan to buy the annihilation of all the Jews. After telling the king how much he would pay, the king granted him permission, and Haman set out to destroy the Jews. After Esther discovered the plot, she knew she had to do something. But no one was allowed to enter into the throne room to see the king unless summoned by name. If she were to simply show up, she risked her life. Mordecai, knowing that she risked her life by keeping silent as well, reassured her with these words: "And who knows whether you have not come to the kingdom for such a time as this?" (Esther 4:14 ESV). Esther, full of courage, sent her reply: "Then I will go to the king, though it is against the law, and if I perish, I perish" (Esther 4:16 ESV).

The courage residing in Esther was not her own, but she knew the God it belonged to, and if she had learned anything in her life, it was that God was the author of her story. Esther was willing to lay down her own life so thousands of her kindred would survive. Just as Mordecai refused to bow down to anyone but God, Esther refused to bow down to fear.

Esther valiantly risked it all to enter the king's presence. Miraculously, she remained in favor with the king, and he not only spared her life but told her to ask whatever it was she wanted of him, and it would be granted. In a time and culture in which it was unacceptable to speak up, Esther skillfully revealed her story to the king, telling who she was by heritage and who she was presently by her faith in God. She knew that sharing her past was exceedingly risky, but as Mordecai had spoken over her, she was born for such a time as this.

Esther found herself in a place she never thought she would be, but she used her painful past and her present testimony to save thousands of people. As followers of Christ, we have the potential to have the same eternal impact on the world if we choose to say no to fear and yes to offering our stories to the King, so He can use them however He might in order to save thousands from a lifetime away from God. There is so much at stake, so many lives being hunted, destroyed, and torn apart by the enemy. So many people all over the world are being deceived by Satan into believing that God, if He is even real, is not present or good or active in our lives. We were born for such a time as this. We were born to live a life that honors God in the valleys and on the mountaintops, outside the gates of the city and in the palace walls with the king. So when our time comes to speak up about what God has done in our lives, how He has *saved* us, how He has *restored* us, and how He *loves* us … we can do so boldly, without fear. It's time. You were born for this. I was born for this. We were born to tell the world, *"I know Him"* in such a time as this.

It is important that as we remember Esther's story, we don't glaze over the part of her past before she became the queen, before she was honored for her beauty and surpassed all the competition by the favor God had given her. Before all this, she was an orphan. Her parents had passed away, and this young girl was raised by an uncle who took her in as his own. Anyone who has lost a loved one can relate to this, especially if it was a parent. We don't know much about how young she was when she moved in with her uncle Mordecai or if she struggled with anger and fear, or wrestled with God over the way her life was going. It is safe to say, however, that it was not always easy. It is safe to say there were days that the pain was so great and the doubt so vast that trusting that God was *still good* was much easier said than done. And I know so many people with the same kind of experiences, who wrestle with past experiences of pain—and probably will for the majority of their lives. However, any chance they get to use their stories to bring hope to the hopeless and be light in the darkness, they boldly share *all of it.* They believe that when God says He uses what was intended to harm us and makes it for our benefit, *He meant it* (Genesis 50:20). They know that souls are at risk, and they plant their feet firmly in the faith they have held onto for dear life, sharing whatever they need to advance the gospel. Telling their stories in hopes of bringing one more heart into a relationship with Christ and to break the chains of one more individual, trapped in shame and guilt, by the groundbreaking power of the cross.

After countless experiences of persecution, in Paul's letter to the church at Philippi, he wrote something that should remain at the forefront of every storyteller's mind: "I want you to know, brothers, that what has happened to me has really served to advance the gospel" (Philippians 1:12 ESV). That is it, short and sweet. That is why we rise to the challenge, why we boldly share what God has done in our lives and the mountains He has moved. Those who share a piece of their lives, a piece of their hearts, and vulnerably become an open book for the world to read, become ambassadors of the gospel. Whether you are in the midst of a trial or have managed to make it through to the other side, when you accept the task of sharing why you know God is here, He is real, and He is good, you have determined that whatever has happened or is happening is solely for the sake of advancing the gospel.

This is an immediate perspective shift, one that is counter-culture and most certainly not the norm. The circumstances are the same. The loss is still loss. The pain remains. The grief is still unfathomable. The anxiety is still threatening. *But it now has a purpose.* There is a plan. The plan is to believe that God is here, He is real, and He is good through it all. And no matter how the circumstance ends up, how this season turns out, when it is our time to share, we stand and say even then, "God is here. God is real. And He is good."

Some people think we have to wait until after the storm is over to share what God is doing, especially if we are unsure of the ending. But one of the most powerful illustrations of someone sharing that God is on the move comes again from Joshua, who was standing just outside of what was to be a huge battle in determining the future of the Israelites.

As Moses' successor, Joshua was leading the Israelites into the promised land. After all they had been through, they had but one thing in their way: Jericho. It was a city surrounded by a fortress, a solid wall of protection for those inside. The generation that had escaped slavery in Egypt had all but died out, and this new generation knew that God had given them this land, but their doubts were about as high as the wall that prohibited their entrance. It was there, just outside of Jericho, that their faithful leader, Joshua, realized the importance of acknowledging God's presence before the storm even arrived:

> When Joshua was by Jericho, he lifted up his eyes and looked, and behold, a man was standing before him with his drawn sword in his hand. And Joshua went to him and said to him, "Are you for us, or for our adversaries?" And he said, "No; but I am the commander of the army of the Lord. Now I have come." And Joshua fell on his face to the earth and worshiped and said to him, "What does my lord say to his servant?" And the commander of the Lord's army said to Joshua, "Take off your sandals

from your feet, for the place where you are standing is holy." And Joshua did so. (Joshua 5:13-15 ESV)

Right now, wherever we are in our lives, if we have the Spirit of God dwelling within us, the very place we are standing is *holy ground*. It is not holy because of how righteous we are or because of the location in which we are standing, but because of the God who is moving *in* and *through* us. Before we walk into the fire, *He is there*. He is *on the move* before we even open our eyes in the morning. He is *breaking strongholds* while we sleep and dream. The presence of God is physically *with* us when we find ourselves in the fire (Daniel 3:25). When we are overcome with sorrow and uncertainty, He remains steadfast, anchoring our hope in the resurrected Christ (Hebrews 6:19). The stories of people who have made it through the trial, those who have emerged from the pit victoriously because of Christ, are powerful and inspiring. But we also need to be sharing those stories of when God was *with us* before He lifted us out of the pit (Psalm 40:2). The world is desperate to also hear from followers of God who experienced His goodness when nothing about their lives or circumstance was good. Or that when they were in a season of peace, His presence was all the more tangible, right where they were in life.

If you and I carry the breath of the living God in us, then it doesn't matter where we are; the place we are standing is *holy ground*. God is moving in and through us if we are high school students, on the basketball team, or preparing for college. God is empowering us to do something incredible for the kingdom if we are rocking babies at two in the morning or chasing toddlers all day. He is building a foundation of faith if we are doing shift work all day and pouring our hearts out at night. He is asking everything of us and nothing less.

The enemy wants us to miss out on the experiences God has for us right where we are because if we were to truly believe that right where we are is *holy ground*, it would change everything. Lives would be impacted for eternity, not a minute wasted for the sake of the gospel. There is so much God has for us, just within our reach if we would only open our eyes to see. In his book, *The Pursuit of God*, A. W. Tozer writes, "Why do we consent to abide all our days just outside the Holy of Holies, and never enter at all to look upon God?" Later in that same book he emphasizes on what exactly we are just missing: "God himself is here waiting our response to His presence."[14]

The weight of that reality rings that it is *we,* not God, who are distant. He is *waiting* for us to respond to Him moving mountains in our lives, breathing life into dead bones, and splitting seas so we can walk into the future He has for us. We are here for such a time as this, and it is our responsibility not to waste a single moment, a single line in our stories. There is far too much at risk. The time is *now* because the ground is *holy.*

---

[14] A. W. Tozer, *The Pursuit of God,* (Harrisburg, PA., Christian Publications, Inc., 1948), Chapter 3

The Gathering

A couple of months after beginning my journey with #IKnowHim, the stories we shared online began to spread throughout our community, and the response was *unreal*. Friends and strangers alike were encouraging us and sharing their excitement. People told me they were praying for me and those serving with me, and my heart overflowed. I was praying daily for affirmation, that this was what I was supposed to be doing. And God kept revealing that yes, this crazy, scary, overwhelming task was where my burden lay, and it was my responsibility to steward. He began to move in mighty ways, from tiny details to incredible provision. His presence was steadfast through it all.

While I was overjoyed that people were getting the message and understanding the vision, I was constantly in awe at how fast God was moving and how He seemed to just breathe life into #IKnowHim and make it into something more than I could have ever dreamed. I found myself repeatedly visiting the passage of scripture in Ezekiel 37 where the breath of God brought life not just to a new heart, but to literally lifeless bones. "Then he said to me, 'Prophesy over these bones, and say to them, O dry bones, hear the word of the Lord. Thus says the Lord God to these bones: Behold, I will cause breath to enter you, and you shall live" (Ezekiel 37:4–5 ESV). And the prophet does what God instructed, and the bones, rattling, come together. Then God instructs Ezekiel to prophesy once more, this time, for life over the dead bones. "So I prophesied as he commanded me, and the breath came into them, and they lived and stood on their feet, an exceedingly great army" (Ezekiel 37:10 ESV).

As the excitement grew, so did the hope that old, dry bones—defeated and barren—would awaken by the breath of God eager to join the army of the saints, proclaiming that God is in their midst. This was an army building; I could feel it. Dead bones were coming together. God was breathing life into something that always belonged to Him.

I found myself sitting at a coffee shop one evening. It was late, after my kids had gone to sleep and I was writing and praying and writing some more. A few moments into my work, I began to get emotional about everything that had transpired. I was completely blown away by what God had done with something so seemingly small. I remember praying, "God, I love what you are doing, but *what on earth are you doing?*" I stopped writing and opened my Bible. The Spirit nudged me toward Isaiah, and what I read then has been playing in the background of my mind and heart every day since. That night at that crowded (and cold) coffee shop, God spoke so clearly and so vividly through His Word that I will never forget it. I read from chapter 56 of Isaiah. In the verse the prophet writes:

> The Sovereign LORD declares—he who gathers the exiles of Israel: "I will gather still others to them besides those already gathered." (Isaiah 56:8 ESV)

This was it. In one verse, not even a whole moment after I asked God what He was doing, He had given me an answer. And it was so overwhelmingly simple. And perfect. And powerful. What God was doing with #IKnowHim had absolutely nothing to do with me. It had everything to do with the vision He had given me in my car that day months before. He was *gathering*. He was bringing those who have yet to believe to those that already believe. Through #IKnowHim He was gathering stories that brought people together, Jesus followers *and* those who have not yet taken up the cross. Passionate disciples *and* prodigal sons. Evangelists and the searching. Broken jars of clay and whitewashed tombs. All these people He was bringing together by stories of people experiencing God so that one name would be on their lips while they listened in awe: the name of *Jesus*.

When I think of that image, of the name of Jesus on everyone's lips, my mind instantly goes back to a few years ago in college when I had a similar experience, when everyone's mind landed on God at the same time. I was at a large university, in an auditorium full of about 250 students. We were in an astronomy class. Although I'm sure about five or six people were genuinely interested in astronomy, for the most part it is safe to say we were in the class because we were terrible at any science that involved cells and scientific methods, and this class was the perfect answer to meet our science requirement for graduation. (And all the art majors said *amen*.)

It was one of the first few days in class, and from the time I read the syllabus on the very first day, my stomach was in knots. From the text on the syllabus, I understood that on this specific day, we were to have read the chapter over the origin of the world and be prepared for that lecture. (My hands are getting sweaty just remembering this.) You see, I had been a believer for several years, and the last few years of high school, I had the incredible privilege of being mentored by our youth pastor, who was extremely passionate about apologetics, and the importance of knowing not only what you believe but also why you believe it. From the knot in my stomach and the lump in my throat, I knew that God was asking me to stand up in front of this massive auditorium and speak on His behalf—not that He needed me to, by any means, but so I had the opportunity to tell the world that I knew Him, when it was certainly going to cost me. Little did I know in all those years of studying apologetics that I was being prepared for this moment.

The night before the class, I couldn't sleep. My heart sunk with fear, and my hands were sweaty and shaky. Who was I, a freshman at a huge university, to speak for God, facing an esteemed professor in front of 250 students? Though my fear grew throughout the night, so did my faith. God had put a fire in my bones before I was even created to speak truth and grace and to share the gospel so that others might *know* Him. I began to think of why He would have me do this, to stand up and speak out. It wasn't to argue with the professor (which I'll ashamedly admit I was decent at in high school). It was because there were students in that lecture hall with me who, although I didn't know their names or their stories, I knew were being told that they were here simply because we evolved from stardust, and if they had never heard the gospel, they had no reason to believe otherwise. I began to think that maybe the time was now for them to hear, maybe for the first time, that they are here because *God* has created them in His love for them. Not one of them is simply part of a larger coincidence, here only to breathe in and out and then to die one day following a meaningless existence. No, God was asking me to speak up for the purpose that He put on their hearts. He was asking me to bring the name of Jesus to the forefront of that classroom so that someone out there, even if just *one*, would begin to consider that God is *real*. And He is *here*. And He is *good*. Maybe just *one student* would find someone who followed Jesus and would ask him or her about how to begin a relationship with this God who created him or her *on purpose—for His purpose*.

The time came the next day when our professor began her lecture on the star that exploded and how the entire world and everything in it evolved from those remnants. Stomach nauseous and hands sweating, I raised my hand (something no one had yet done for the first few classes, even). Praying fervently in the back of my mind for God to speak through me, I began our conversation. The only thing I could think about was the students who needed to hear the truth. I didn't know who they were, but I was fighting for them. I have no idea what I said, but I remembered one of the most important things I learned all my years of studying was to simply ask the questions and leave the rest to God. I began to backtrack, asking where it all originated from. I started from each term she used and asked "Okay, where did the material for that originate?" This went on for a while. Finally, after what felt like forever, we got to the original molecule, the very base of that original star. And I remember looking at her, and the rest of the class, knowing she had nowhere to turn but the inevitable. Praying that my words would be seasoned with grace, I told her, "I am most certainly not trying to be disrespectful. But I know that there are students in here who don't know why they are here. And I can't sit back and let them be told that it is because they are the result of stardust. My last question is this: Where did that original molecule, the one that you say expanded into the star, and so on ... where did that originate? It had to come from somewhere."

And then something happened that I will *never* forget. The room was so silent you could hear a pin drop. It felt like a movie. I held my breath (even though I don't think I had ever breathed the whole time really), and all over the auditorium, students began to whisper in their seats: *"Jesus."*

"Jesus," I heard from the row behind me. And again, "Jesus. Jesus. Jesus." All whispered just above a hush, but just loud enough so others could hear, all over the room.

Jesus. The name that Acts 4:12 says is the only name under heaven that can save us. *Jesus.* The name that Philippians 2:9–11 tells us is the name at which every knee will bow. *Jesus.* The name that causes demons to flee (Acts 16:18) and paralytics to rise up and walk (Acts 3:6). *Jesus.* The name that brings the dead to life. *Jesus.* The name by which *all things* were created, as told in Colossians 1:16.

And then the professor ended class twenty minutes early. And I have never been the same. And I hope that at least one person will never be the same either. I'll never know. But what I do know is that feeling of Jesus being the thing on everyone's mind was so incredibly powerful, and that is *exactly* what He is asking of me now. To challenge people to share stories that draw attention to the One who heals, the One who breaks chains, the One who moves mountains, the One who forgives, the One who *saves.*

The point of these #IKnowHim stories, of this gathering, is not to draw attention to the storytellers but to the author of the stories. The goal is to shed light on stories of God moving and healing, rescuing and restoring, so that people are confronted with the Author of *all* stories.

One other thing I know is that the Holy Spirit has the power to say whatever needs to be said to whomever needs to hear it, regardless of what I say. Matthew 10:20 (ESV) says, "For it is not you who speak, but the Spirit of your Father speaking through you." It is 100 percent possible that I absolutely butchered the majority of our conversation that day. But the Holy Spirit did the work, and in the moments that others needed to hear God, they did. And that is all that matters. When

God asks us to do something, most of the time, it is really difficult. But thank God that it is not left to us to do or say the right things. Of us, He merely asks for trust, which results in our obedience. And our obedience opens the door for the Spirit to move hearts and mountains to get people face-to-face with the God who loves them.

When people are confronted with something that could only have been accomplished by the power of God, they are confronted with the reality that God is real, He is here, and He is good. If stories like this were to catch on, the name of Jesus would be on our lips more than on Sunday, and people would begin to really believe that He is *in our midst* (Zephaniah 3:17). He is not just in our churches. He is in our homes, our places of work, and our hearts. His presence can fill any room and change even the most hostile atmosphere. There is nowhere He cannot reach and no one He cannot pursue.

Again in his book *The Pursuit of God,* A. W. Tozer wrote, "Men do not know that God is here. What a difference it would make if they knew."[15] That is the power of the gospel. That is the power of the person of Jesus. What if we began seeing more stories of God on the move than of war, terrorism, and greed? People would begin to hear. They would begin to consider. They would begin to *believe.* Then *they* would begin to share.

It is time to watch God gather. It is time be a part of the gathering. It is time for *me* to join the gathering, to join my fellow brothers and sisters, Jesus followers from all around the world, to use the words of our testimony to wage war on darkness. As I issue the challenge for believers to boldly share their stories, I am going to accept the challenge to share mine all along the way—about how He saved me, how He provides for me, and how He speaks straight to my heart fire for His Word in my bones.

If ever there has been a time to tell the world that you know Him, it is now. Tell your family. Tell your friends. Tell your coworkers. Tell *your enemy.* Tell them how you have experienced God in your life. Share

---

[15] A. W. Tozer, *The Pursuit of God,* (Harrisburg, PA., Christian Publications, Inc., 1948), Chapter 3

your story with your community or on the #IKnowHim blog as a first step. Just tell someone. Light someone else's flame. The time is now.

It doesn't matter what you have done or what has been done to you. All that matters is what God has done *for* you. Will you join us? Will you join the fight to overcome darkness? Will you add your flame to the fire that is spreading all around the world bearing the name of Jesus? We are *done* being overcome by fear. We are saying *yes* to bravery and courage. Our armor is on. We are joining our fellow soldiers. Our battle cry?

"I know Him."

Have you ever thought about how encompassing God's plan is? I think that one part of His plan in this season of my life is time. Literally— time of the day. My sister died in the early morning hours of a Sunday, exactly seven days after my birthday and only five days before my youngest daughter's birthday. After she passed away, we all sat in the waiting room at the hospital, not grasping the reality of our time there being finished. Nobody wanted to leave. In the initial minutes, and maybe even hours of a loved one dying, I don't think the finality of everything is comprehended. We knew that there was nothing left for us to do in the hospital, but leaving meant that my sister was really gone, and that wasn't too appealing to any of us. She was my little sister, of course, but the rest of the story is what made everyone sick to their stomachs. She was twenty-nine, the mother of a seven-year-old little girl, married four months ago to her soulmate, and gave birth to her son only days before.

It was dark outside still, the night sky clinging to its final few hours, but it felt dark in that waiting room, too. Almost too dark. Definitely too dark to be able to see our next steps. I don't know how much time went by crying in the arms of each other in the waiting room, but eventually each of us piled into the lobby's elevator and descended four floors back into reality. I wanted those elevator doors to open and awaken me from my dream. Kind of like those dreams you have when you're falling and you wake up just before you hit the ground. I was ready to wake up, but in the back of my head, I knew it wasn't going to happen, because it was too late; I had already hit the ground.

The elevator doors slid open, and we reluctantly walked through the halls we had entered through a few hours ago, when my sister was still alive. Each step we took toward the dark night outside felt heavy. I remember getting in my truck, driving to my sister's home. The dark night outside illuminated by the traffic lights that served no purpose on the early-morning empty streets. I can remember feeling guilty for leaving my sister by herself in that hospital room, not yet grasping that it was just her body. I remember the awkwardness of driving to their home with no real purpose but to sit silently, crying.

At work, we have sleepless nights at the fire station—nights where the tones sound for a call every time your head hits the pillow. Those nights are memorable, mostly because of how they make you feel the following day—hazy and unfocused. The sleeplessness of this night was different. I wasn't sleepy; I wasn't tired.

There were maybe ten or fifteen of us in a room able to seat about five. Some were standing, and some were pacing. I was sitting next to my wife, uncontrollable tears flowing from both our eyes. Our two girls were sleeping in the bed my sister had lain down in just a few hours ago after tucking her girls in for bed. My oldest daughter's head lay on the pillow that my sister's head had lain on just after kissing her husband goodnight, unknowingly for the final time.

We sat in the darkness, silently crying. Everyone muffled their sorrow, in fear of waking my sister's daughter, who had kissed her mother—her best friend—good night and peacefully slept through the night, clueless of the war on the other side of her door. We knew that, eventually, she would awaken to a new life, and we were preparing our minds and our hearts for that moment. Through the brokenness on my brother-in-law's face, you could see the fear of the conversation that lay ahead.

By now, the darkness of the night became a small comfort. I didn't want the sun to rise. The sun rising meant that we would have to begin to deal with everything. Right now, in the darkness, we could just cry. As the light just began to push the darkness from the east sky, beginning to drown the light of the stars, my niece woke from her sleep. As my parents and my brother-in-law walked into her room, we sat in the dark house awaiting the reaction to the horror that was being unveiled a few feet away.

I consider myself a strong man. I have heard cries of pain and anguish before, but nothing could have prepared me for the screams that were about to echo off the walls of this small house. I had stood from my seat and for some reason felt the need to stand in front of my niece's bedroom door, almost like a guard prepared to keep anything from entering. There was no need to guard the door; this home was filled with family. It was just instinct, I guess. The sound of a child being told that her mother is gone is crushing and will break the strongest of men. I was not exempt. It was the first time in my life that a sound literally hurt me—broke me, emotionally and physically. I became weak. I couldn't bear the pain of listening to the cries. Most of the others were still sitting in the darkness. Cries of brokenness, helplessness, and despair depleted the oxygen in the room, making it impossible to breathe. I walked to the front door and stepped onto the porch, now guarding the house. It was a pointless guard because we had all felt defeated already, unable to be broken any more than what we were. I stood on the front porch looking to the east sky, giving up on wiping away tears.

I resorted to training from my job in trying to control my breathing and my heart. One deep breath. Hold it. Several small exhales. It was pointless. It wasn't as much the death but the story and the remnants of it that were piercing.

The sun was rising over the houses, and the west Texas sky was painted in color. A new day was beginning—a new normal for our family. It was a sunrise in every sense and meaning of the word. For hours, we had dreaded it, but it was here. I looked to the sky, literally watching the darkness of night disappear. The cool September air outside made it a little easier to breathe. The sun rising in the sky was a glimpse into the realization in the coming days that life would go on. The darkest night of our lives was over, the storm had shattered us and broken us, and now it was time to begin the arduous task of dealing with the remnants and its path of destruction. I kept telling myself, in my head, that I could handle this, but I felt more like I was trying to convince myself of it rather than actually believing it.

Still standing on the front porch, I watched the painted morning sky transform to a beautiful fall morning. It was a Sunday morning, so it was still quiet. Families were still asleep in their beds or waking for church. Sunday mornings in West Texas are a little quieter than other days and slower paced. I was jealous of the people in the homes around us. Their nights were normal. The spotlight of God's great plan wasn't shining on them last night. They were waking to another day, not consumed with brokenness, anger, and regret. Why us?

Eventually, I took one last deep breath and went back inside, walking into a journey that I am still on. The next hours, days, and weeks were hectic and hazy, leaving little time for reflection. However, every morning since, the sun has risen. The sky has been painted by God and the darkness ushered out. Every morning I wake early for work. I'm either going to the fire station or returning home as the sun is rising. This morning, I watched the sun rise, holding a coffee in my hand. I realized that it has been the most constant thing since the day my sister went to heaven. I remembered how broken I felt that morning at her home, watching it rise, and I looked at where I am now. I still feel broken, but the morning sun, to me, brings hope. I know that God has a plan, and tomorrow is never guaranteed. I am learning to put my faith in His plan. I do believe, though, that watching the sun rise that morning was part of His plan for me. I knew that as I would walk through the next days, weeks, months, and years, I would see that sunrise and feel its hope and consistency and God's plan at work. Remember that we are not in control, and God's plan is at work right now. Life is filled with storms, and each dark sky presents differently. However, the difference in appearances do not influence the weight of the clouds hovering above. The pages of the Bible are saturated with storms and battles won and lost. I find comfort in knowing that God has the power to turn tragedy into triumph—bringing beauty from the ashes. Every morning when I wake, I still process the fact that I have lost my little sister. I have learned to find a new normal, but we continue the task of overhauling the destruction of that dark night.

The first spring since her passing has seen the blossom of flowers, the leaves return to the branches of the trees, and life reemerge from the cold of winter. A new season is upon us, and God's plan turns a new page. I have climbed a rugged path to get to where I am today, but my footing has not failed. The path has been impossible to see at times, but I have learned that it is not as important to be able to see the path as it is to have faith that the path is forged.

The same God who delivered Jonah from the depths of the ocean to the safety of dry land; the one who allowed David to conquer a giant;

the one whose Son calmed the seas with His voice and walked on water has shown Himself to me.

I was thirty-six years old when God gave me my storm, and I was thirty-six years old when I felt the presence and power of God. I would love to say that there is a happy ending, but the ending is not yet written. I press on through every day with a newly found faith in a God that can conquer the darkness. This storm has changed my life. Beauty from ashes—triumph from tragedy.

God has a plan, and it is at work in your life every single second of every single day. The reality is that, at times, through our limited vision and finite comprehension, that plan sucks. However, if we are able to detach, surround ourselves with the right people, keep our faith, and appreciate that the God that brought us here will deliver us from here, triumph will conquer all.

God bless.

#IKnowHim story submitted by Kyle Joy
Third Strand
www.thirdstrand.foundation

Epilogue

How to Tell Your Story

There is no greater time than the present to share stories of God on the move. However, it can be overwhelming to get caught up in how to even begin sharing our stories. Let me begin by saying this: *there is no wrong way to tell someone what God has done for you.* There is so much freedom in knowing all we have to offer is our love for Jesus, and it is He who will accomplish the rest because it is Christ alone who brings hope and salvation. Our words are powerful, yes, but don't forget that Revelation 12:11 tells us that it is by *the blood and of the Lamb and the word of our testimonies* that darkness is conquered. We must never forget that we have a story to tell and that story is His; it is the story of what He has done for us. We can never mistakenly tell someone that we love Jesus. What He has done in our own hearts and our own lives will make sharing His story all the more natural.

If we offer our time and our story to God and pray that He would give us the words to speak, He is faithful to do just that (Luke 12:12) and will even speak on our behalf. That being said, there are some concrete and effective ways to share your story with people you come across in your daily life. These are only tips to hopefully make this incredible task seem a little less daunting. Keep in mind this list is not exhaustive! The ways to communicate how God has moved in your life are limitless with open eyes, a grateful heart, and a courageous spirit.

First, pray that God would give you opportunities to share your story. Then, be diligent in looking for open doors in daily conversations. He will be so delighted to honor this request. When you come across people in conversation and they share something they are struggling with, take a deep breath, pray for God to speak for you, and begin to share your story. An easy way to transition would be to say something such as: "I am so sorry you are going through that. Can I share something personal from my life that might encourage you?"

Immediately following those words, say nothing else. You have extended the invitation. (But be ready to continue, because who is going to say no to *hope*!) After the person agrees, begin sharing your story by implementing some of these prompts to assist you in chronicling the highlights of your testimony regarding what is relevant to that person.

- Share when an influential season or moment occurred in your life.
- Share what the circumstances were.
- Share what you felt, prayed, needed, etc.
- Share how you experienced God (His presence, provision, faithfulness, etc.). *This is the most important piece!*
- Share a scripture that reflects what you experienced regarding God's character.

Telling your story this way gives people looking for hope concrete details about how someone they know experienced that God is real, God is here, and God is good. The next step is to open up the conversation by putting the ball in their court. Let them ask questions, and pray for an opportunity to offer them help in beginning a new life in Christ. Conclude your conversation by asking how you can specifically be praying for them as they walk through this season, and follow through with your commitment to pray for them.

In addition to sharing your story with those around you, I want to extend a special invitation to submit your story to the #IKnowHim blog, where others can be inspired by your boldness to share and encouraged to pursue what it means to know God in their own lives if they are not yet believers. This is a great way to use our resources with technology and social media as a means of furthering the good news that in Jesus there is hope and new life for all. If you are interested in submitting a story for review to be featured on the blog, visit:

www.iknowhim.us

My prayer is that this would not simply be another book you have read but one that results in action. I hope you are inspired and encouraged to be a light in the darkness by sharing that God is real, He is here, and He is good to a world that so desperately longs to hear how you know that is true. Let's join the fight together and let "I Know Him" be the banner we carry as we overcome the enemy by the blood of the Lamb and the words of our testimonies.

Grace and peace,
Rachel Sweatt

Acknowledgments

There are countless individuals that come to mind when I think about who played a part in the shaping of this book, helping me steward this vision, and kindly offering wisdom and correction every step of the way. Please know that if you are reading this and you had any conversation with me, prayed for me and my family, or offered encouragement throughout this process, I am beyond thankful to partner with you in this ministry. I too have prayed for you and hope that God grants you the blessing of seeing the fruit of this labor in your lives abundantly.

My first thank you is to the "Him" in our title, the God above all, and my sweet, sweet Savior. This is an offering to You and for You. Thank You for allowing me the privilege of watching *You* gather people to the beautiful name of Jesus, and breathing new life and hope into this broken mess of a world. Let it always be You, God. What a privilege it is to be poured out by You and for Your glory.

To my better half, the love of my life, and the dad to my *E-tribe*, thank you doesn't feel quite adequate. Thank you for the late-night snacks while I worked, the hours you gifted me to flee from the beautiful noise in our home so I could focus, and the countless prayers you lifted up on my behalf. There is no one else I would rather serve Jesus with than you. Let's do this forever, okay! Xoxo.

Thank you to my sweet, crazy, beautiful boys. Emmett and Easton, even though you didn't know it, you were incredibly patient with your mama during this writing season, and I hope you know how much it means to me to share this with you. I pray that the legacy we are building together never ceases to fill your hearts with assurance that

God loves you and made each of you to do sacred, holy things for His glory. You both love people so well. Thank you for teaching me more about what it means to know God every day. I'm so proud of you. I love you more than you'll ever know. I'm so thankful for you.

Thank you to our incredible family and our parents (Pat, Zane, Cindy, and Tirk) for believing in me and investing in this ministry. Your support means the world to me. Thank you for praying for me, my family, and our ministry as a family from before we were even born!

To my sweet sisters in the faith who have lifted my arms throughout this journey from day one, from my friends at Hillside to my friends praying for me from afar—the Lord has heard every prayer, and I am so grateful. Amy and Sydney, thank you both for being mentors in the faith and for loving me and praying me through some of the hardest seasons of growth in my life thus far. I am so thankful for your holy friendships. I want you in my tribe forever! Thank you for sacrificing so much time to help me proofread these pages and every suggestion you gave to make this book the best offering it could be.

Thank you to Ismael Burciaga of Burciaga and Co. for believing and supporting this ministry from its earliest days with the blog design as well as the book design! Thank you to Blake Cartrite of Simple and Historic for creating the most stunning video (beautifully written by Sydney Clark) about what it means to know God. (If you're reading this and haven't seen the video, you can watch it at www.iknowhim.us!)

Thank you to Patcine McAnual, Ken Bundy, Sydney Clark, and Kyle Joy for allowing your stories to be featured in this book. Also, thank you to every person who has shared a story with us online. It is a privilege to share the gospel with you!

Thank you to our church family, our pastors and elders, and my mentors past and present for pouring into us, praying for us, and serving Jesus with all you have. Every second of your outpouring is making an eternal difference. *Thank you!*

Resources

Charles Spurgeon, *Spurgeon's Sermons Volume 06: 1860,* (Ontario, Canada, Devoted Publishing, 2017,) *140*

Saint Augustine, *Confessions,* (London, England, Penguin Group, 1961), 23

C. S. Lewis, *Mere Christianity,* (New York, New York, HarperOne, 1952), 176

"Americans Have Little Doubt God Exists," Gallup, accessed October 21,2016, http://www.gallup.com/poll/20437/americans-little-doubt-god-exists.aspx

Oswald Chambers, *My Utmost For His Highest: Updated Edition,* (Grand Rapids, Michigan, Discovery House, 1992) 7/6

C. S. Lewis, *Letters of C.S. Lewis,* (New York, New York, Harper-Collins, 1966) 220

Joseph Henry Thayer, D.D., *A Greek-English Lexicon of the New Testament,* (Edinburgh, T. & T. Clark, 1890) 392

"World Watch List," Open Doors, Accessed November 3, 2016, https://www.opendoorsusa.org/christian-persecution/world-watch-list/

"Christian persecution reached record high in 2015," CNN, accessed January 1, 2017, http://www.cnn.com/2016/01/17/world/christian-persecution-2015/

"The Scandal of Election 2016," The LPM Blog, Accessed October 18, 2016, http://blog.lproof.org/2016/10/the-scandal-of-election-2016.html

"About," Afshin Ziafat, Accessed October 9 2016, http://www.afshinzi-afat.com/about.php

C.S. Lewis, *The Weight of Glory*, (New York, New York, Harper Collins, 1949) 26

A. W. Tozer, *The Pursuit of God*, (Harrisburg, PA., Christian Publications, Inc., 1948)

Printed in the United States
By Bookmasters